PRAISE FOR *THE X AND Y OF BUY*

"Your greatest competitive advantage is to understand your customer. In this informative, entertaining, and highly relevant book, Elizabeth Pace lets you in on the most important customer knowledge of all: how men and women make buying decisions. This is a great book!"

Joe Calloway
Author, *Becoming A Category of One*

"An enjoyable and beneficial read, appropriate for all businesses with a gender-diverse sales force or gender-diverse clients. If you have a son or daughter, a father or mother, or a sister or brother, you know that men and women think and react differently, but you probably don't understand why or know how best to adapt to each. Elizabeth Pace presents well considered, scientifically based advice in an entertaining and easy to digest format to enable men and women to better tailor their business sales and marketing to each gender, increasing their individual chance of success and thus your business' efficiency and sales!"

Jennifer J. Fahey
Executive Vice President, Co-Leader,
ARS U.S. Sales and Marketing
Aon Risk Services, Inc.

"*The X and Y of Buy* should be required reading for any student, employee, consultant or executive involved in—or planning on being involved in—promotional activities, whether related to product or service. Gender represents one major, final piece to the sales and marketing puzzle that confounds so many: how does one incorporate gender differences as an unfair advantage? Elizabeth Pace has done a marvelous job of explaining the differences and offering practical approaches."

Stryker Warren Jr.
CEO, Urologix
Healthcare Entrepreneur

"Everyone can benefit from reading this book! It explains human behavior from a scientific standpoint and helps us understand why men and women behave in the sometimes seemingly crazy ways that they do. The examples were perfect, as I laughed out loud at the similarity to experiences I have had at home and in the workplace. The information and strategies presented are widely applicable to dealings with men and women in both business and personal situations."

Laura L. Lawson, MD

"As a counselor and executive coach for over twenty years, I have read countless books about communication, but I found Elizabeth Pace's book *The X and Y of Buy* to be full of original, insightful information that men and women could use in their professional and personal lives. Pace has an excellent grasp on what makes each sex unique, and she delivers that wisdom without judgment and with a desire to help everyone learn how to maximize their ability to be heard and understood."

Ken Cope
Executive Coach, Core Resources, LLC

The
X and Y
of Buy

The
X and Y
of Buy

Sell More and Market Better
by Knowing How the Sexes Shop

Elizabeth Pace

THOMAS NELSON
Since 1798

NASHVILLE   DALLAS   MEXICO CITY   RIO DE JANEIRO   BEIJING

Published in Nashville, Tennessee, by Thomas Nelson. Thomas Nelson is a registered trademark of Thomas Nelson, Inc.

Linda Konner Literary Agency

Thomas Nelson, Inc., titles may be purchased in bulk for educational, business, fund-raising, or sales promotional use. For information, please e-mail SpecialMarkets@ThomasNelson.com.

Library of Congress Cataloging-in-Publication Data

Pace, Elizabeth, 1959–
  The X and Y of buy : sell more and market better by knowing how the sexes shop / Elizabeth Pace.
     p. cm.
  Includes bibliographical references.
  ISBN 978-1-59555-105-4 (hbk.)
  1. Consumers—Psychology. 2. Consumer behavior—Sex differences. 3. Shopping—Sex differences. I. Title.
  HF5415.32.P33 2009
  658.8'342—dc22

                                                      2009014086

Printed in the United States of America
09 10 11 12 13 QW 6 5 4 3 2 1

For all that you do to fill my soul and make my heart sing, I dedicate this book to my family . . .

Carah, I am continually astonished by your focus and creativity—I love you more.

Ally, your sense of the absurd and your huge heart light up my life.

Phil, your wisdom, patience, and strength are my rock. Thank you for always making our marriage vows mean what we said.

contents

Contents

SEX, SALES, AND STEREOTYPES

During my twenty-five plus years in branding, marketing, and sales in the hospital and health care industries, I have studied dozens of sales techniques and programs, all promising to increase sales through identifying and understanding behavioral types. Armed with this information, I *should* be able to communicate the right message, in the right style, at the right time, and with maximum impact to any prospect or client. By using these behavioral models, marketers and salespeople have tried to apply some science to the art of selling.

One big problem: I am not a behavioral psychologist and cannot for the life of me remember the many behavioral types, let alone identify—in the first five minutes of a meeting—my potential customer's innate behavioral patterns. I'm guessing the same is true of many of you too.

Always in search of a better method to connect to my customers, I became intrigued in the mid-1990s with emerging neuroscience that used functional MRI (fMRI) studies to actually trace the activity in the human brain. As these studies rolled out—and continue to, on an accelerated path with enhanced technology—it was astounding to find that the male and female brains respond to many stimuli differently.

Then in March 2002, while on a layover in the Las Vegas airport with my family, I wandered into the airport bookstore. The newly released hardback *The Wonder of Girls* by Michael Gurian caught my eye. I had been traveling nine hours with my daughters, then ages six and four, and was actually beginning to empathize with species that eat their young. Fortunately, I devoured the book instead of my children. Fascinated by the biological explanations of my daughters' and my own forty-something female behavior, I pored through other books that discussed biological gender differences that affect behavior.

Since I have spent my entire professional life in marketing and sales, and I have a female-differentiated brain —which you will learn loves to relate ideas—my brain automatically sifts most information through the "how does this relate to marketing?" filter. Hence the X and Y of Buy idea was born.

I think you'll agree that within two seconds of meeting a new person, you can accurately identify if that individual is male or female, 99.99 percent of the time. Congratulations—you've already won half the battle if your sales strategy hinges not on psychological grouping but on gender-specific differences. I also believe you will find *The X and Y of Buy* tools easier to implement than trying to profile every prospect and client.

You'll recognize the truth of the gender-specific behaviors we'll discuss because you see them every day with your wife, husband, sons, daughters, or coworkers of the same and opposite sexes. I believe it was the writer C. S. Lewis who once perfectly described the transfer of truth from one person to another: "Most people," he explained, "don't need to be told—they just need to be reminded." This book will serve as a sometimes-funny, sometimes-frustrating, all-times-eye-opening reminder for those of us in the business of sales and marketing. It will also take your productivity and profits to another level.

I have divided this book into two parts. The first eight chapters address gender differences and how to target marketing tactics to connect with your male or female audience. In chapters 9 and 10, I explain GenderCycle Selling™, with pragmatic examples of face-to-face selling strategies to men versus women. With most products and services, you can create the best ad campaign in the world, driving customers right to your storefront, but then lose the sale if the salesperson cannot connect and articulate the value of your product.

In the name of full disclosure, there are certainly exceptions to every rule. We can all agree that all men are not the same, and neither are all women identical and the polar opposites of men. There are women with what scientists call "male-differentiated" brains and men with "female-differentiated" brains—yes, there *are* women who enjoy parallel parking their cars. We're not talking about sexual orientation, but rather the thought processes and emotions that drive us. But such exceptions are somewhat rare. By understanding the X and Y of Buy, you'll be more effective with the vast majority of your gender-targeted market. No psychological profiling strategy can give you better odds.

The strength of the X and Y of Buy strategy is simple: whether you are designing a product, advertising a new service, or making the most critical sales presentation of your life, you want your audience to make a choice. The decision maker is either male or female or, at times, the ultimate decision is made by both genders. In every case you must capture your prospect's attention, ignite your prospect's emotions, and inspire him or her to choose you.

The decision to buy is theirs. To best influence their decision, you should understand the brain's decision-making process and the unique ways the process differs for your male and female prospects. It's a strategy few use, but you've likely heard of those who do. They are the ones selling your favorite products and brands to *you*.

PART I

Targeting Hardwired Gender Differences

DIFFERENT BY DESIGN

Men buy; women shop and then
purchase 80 percent of everything.

Shopping for a man's suit? Walk through the main
entrance of Neiman Marcus and—voilà: men's suits in every
color, size, and design are displayed together.

A woman will get a lot more exercise searching for that
new ensemble. She must turn left through the same doors,
away from the men's department, and weave her way through
the maze of perfumes and cosmetics, past the shoes and
purses at the bottom of the escalator. Arriving on the second
floor—devoted entirely to women's apparel—she has the
opportunity to peruse the casual wear and the sequined
formals before finding her favorite designer's section.

Will a woman reach her destination without actually

buying something else on the way? Neiman's thinks not. Would a man ever make it to this remote corner for a designer suit? Not in a million years. Keen retailers like Neiman's know that while women love the search, men love the kill—most find it undesirable, if not downright tedious, to maneuver through a mall. Department stores appeal to men with an easy-in, easy-out layout while also appealing to women, who crave a complex sensory experience while shopping.

Men and women are different. The plumbing is different; the wiring is different. Not better . . . not worse . . . just different. We perceive, think, communicate, and respond to the world differently. To say this in the postfeminist corporate arena has been political suicide. Yet scientists have confirmed that men and women use different parts of their brains and thus behave differently in a host of situations—including the ways we shop, buy, and consume products and services.

As a sales, advertising, or marketing professional, understanding these differences is the key to your success. When you were a child, you were taught the golden rule: treat others as you would like to be treated. But as you grew up, it became evident (often on the school playground) that half of the others—those of the opposite sex—don't respond well to being treated the way that you want to be treated. If you are still treating the other half of your customers the way *you* want to be treated, you are likely missing half (or more) of your market and leaving half (or more) of your sales on the table.

To increase sales, you must understand what uniquely drives your customers, male and female, and maximize your options for communicating with them. Whether you sell tangible products like cars and homes, or intangible products like financial services and business solutions, read on. Understanding the inherent perceptions, motivations, and emotions specific to the X and the Y chromosomes is the most powerful way to increase revenue.

X MARKS THE SPOT

"I Am Because I Shop" was the title of Mallory Keaton's first philosophy paper. As the family's academic under-achiever in the 1980s sitcom *Family Ties*, Mallory expressed the universal teenage girl's cry, "Shop 'til we drop!"

If the drive to buy is written into women's genetic code, scientists should search the X chromosome for the shop-ping gene. Doubly blessed with the X, women now control 83 percent of all consumer purchases. And these products and services are not just soap and paper clips. The majority of home computers, decking materials, new cars, and health care services are purchased by women.[1]

Women have now taken their shopping prowess to the corporate world, where they hold 51 percent of the purchasing manager and agent positions.[2] Women also call most of the shots on benefit purchases, holding the majority of executive positions in human resources.[3]

Not only do women buy most big-ticket items; they have the money to spend. Women now make up 50 percent of the workforce and earn the majority of undergraduate and graduate degrees. For the first time in history, most women over the age of fifty have their own funds. Combine their individual spending power with the fact that women tend to outlive their husbands by about fifteen years, and you'll soon conclude that the money is heading straight into their Coach handbags.[4]

> *"Women are the #1 marketing opportunity."*
> —TOM PETERS, BEST-SELLING AUTHOR

Women are crying out for brands that understand their needs and make purchasing enjoyable. Many salespeople and businesses don't get it. A female attorney recently bemoaned the purchase of her gas-guzzling Suburban, in which she's logged 183,000 miles with her three boys in tow. "I can afford a new car now," she confessed, "but I am determined to drive this one into the ground just to avoid the awful experience of buying a new one."

Marketers who can transform this woman's dread of shopping for a new computer, car, or financial planner into an enjoyable experience will reap substantial rewards.

WHY TARGET Y?

While the above statistics make the case that marketers must do a better job of designing and branding services that appeal to women, there is also ample room to improve your sales with men. Men might be more predictable buyers than women, but they are by no means an easy sale. And to *presume* that you know how to sell to your male customers can have quite painful consequences. While women will tend to let a salesperson down easier, men will call you out and shoot you straight between the eyes if you miss the mark with them. And to ignore their buy buttons is to potentially forgo 20 to 50 percent of your prospects—something no savvy business would do. We'll discuss the specifics of this topic shortly, but for now it should be clear that to increase your bottom line also requires understanding a man's motivation and what triggers his emotional connection to a product or brand. To achieve such a feat for both X and Y, you must first appreciate the unique differences that are hardwired into the male and female brains.

THE EVOLUTION OF THE CONSUMER

When early mankind roamed the earth, they hunted and gathered for something quite specific: food. A day's work was to get the day's meal. Men and women did very different work that was considered equally important to their clan.

THE HUNTER

That Was Then　　　　*This Is Now*

Men hunted in groups, made weapons, and traveled great distances from their homes. They lived a focused, dangerous existence. The man's mission statement was, "Kill my dinner before it kills me!" To thrive, men needed navigation skills, good long-distance and night vision, and spatial aptitude. Strength and a heightened fight-or-flight response defined the survivors. Hunting was a strategic exercise requiring quick decisions, distinct roles, rules, and hierarchy among the group. And it required absolute silence with zero tolerance for emotional displays.

What were the women doing? They were keeping the campfires burning, chasing the children away from the fires, protecting the camp from snakes and other predators, listening for thunder in the distance, and providing care to the sick. Because there were no tools to puree food, each child would be nursed until four years of age, when he or she had the teeth and digestive system to manage the diet of fresh boar, nuts, and berries. Our gatherer ancestors made clothes from animal hides, organized the society, and foraged food for each day's meals. They stored food for the winter or the frequent occasions when the men did not come home with the kill. Anthropologists estimate that women provided at least half of the food for their clans. And in this era devoid of scientific explanations, women had the elevated status of the mystical creators of life.

What traits were necessary for a woman to ensure her clan's survival? To start, a great sense of smell, taste, hearing, and peripheral vision. Women negotiated and settled arguments in the clan, so they had to be able to weigh many issues. While men had to have quick, explosive energy, women needed stamina to get through the long days and the nights interrupted by nursing babies. The hunter-man concentrated on that day's kill; the gatherer-woman had to plan for the longer term and was the original queen of multitasking. This nomadic way of life—following the food source season to season—continued for hundreds of thousands of years.

THE GATHERER

That Was Then   *This Is Now*

Along Comes Mary

With the 1960s came more change in America than witnessed by any prior generation. The dawning of the technology era coincided with the civil rights movement, the Vietnam War, the sexual revolution, and the women's movement. The FDA's approval of "the pill" in 1960 and the passage of the Equal Pay Act of 1963 were catalysts propelling women into "male" professions.

In America and a few other countries today, men and women have comparable educations and relatively equal opportunity. And for the first time in history, we are competing for the same jobs. Yet we come to these positions with different perspectives and innate skills hardwired into our brains that define much of who we are. Only through understanding the primary differences can we unleash the economic power of gender diversity.

DESIGNER GENES

We've come a long way since the turn of the twentieth century, when early brain scientists believed that a head circumference of fewer than fifty-two centimeters indicated a lack of intellectual performance. We now know that the structural gender differences of the brain that endow men and women with innate abilities are determined not by brain size but by the brain's efficiency, connectivity, and intensity during activities.

"We do not need to ask for the head circumference of women of genius—they do not exist."
—BAYERTHAL, 1911

For example, in general, a man's brain is like a file cabinet. Everything has a file. The job has a file, the wife has a file, the kids have a file, golf has a file, and tools have a file (sometimes a very big file). Here's the first and most important man rule: *the files never touch*. When a man contemplates his financial future, with the focus of a laser he very carefully pulls the "money" file, methodically sorts through it, and replaces it without stirring another file. A man zeros in on the task at hand. He has very specific and highly developed brain regions located on the right hemisphere, which is the larger of the two in the male brain and the source for spatial reasoning. Depending on his current focus, he generally uses the right or the left hemisphere—but not both simultaneously. As a result, a man's brain structure allows him to separate his emotions from a problem, act quickly, and move on to the next specific activity.

Picture a woman's brain as a large table. Her files are all laid out in groups touching each other. During the meeting with their financial planner, the husband is a bit surprised when his wife says, "Yes, that is a good point, but you have to think about your Aunt Janet and her failing health when you consider our next five years." His "Aunt Janet" file is not even in the same file drawer as the money file, if the file exists at all. The woman's brain is like a searching lighthouse—seeing, processing, and connecting all things on a 24/7 basis. Ruben Gur, a neuroscientist at the University of Pennsylvania, found that while men can zone out, taking brief mental naps in front of the TV, for example, women's brains are constantly working. There is about 15 percent more blood flow in the female brain than in the male, lighting up more areas in the female brain than the male brain at a given moment.[5]

The first and most important woman rule is that *every file in the female brain relates to all of the other files.*

In a woman's brain, the left hemisphere has 11 percent more neurons for language skills than a man's.[6] The corpus callosum, which connects and facilitates communication between the two hemispheres, is 23 percent larger in women, relative to brain size.[7] This strong connection is considered to be a logical explanation for women's heightened senses, social awareness, and ability to connect seemingly random files to each other.

It doesn't seem fair, but as we age, our brain shrinks noticeably in areas where we are least proficient to begin with. Men lose their brain tissue in the frontal and temporal lobes—the areas associated with feeling and thinking. By age fifty men also lose up to 20 percent of their neurons in the corpus callosum, the region that provides connections between the two hemispheres. Women lose brain tissue later in the aging process but lose it where they are already most challenged—in the viso-spatial area.[8] This explains why Grandma has problems remembering where she parked the car at the grocery store, while Grandpa grows crankier and less articulate with the salesperson. (See the chart below for a breakdown of the primary differences we've just discussed.)

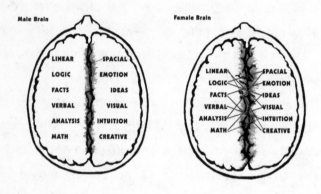

	Brain Structure in Men	Brain Structure in Women
Side by Side	**Right** hemisphere is larger than left. Men use either the right hemisphere *or* the left hemisphere during a specific activity.	**Left** hemisphere is larger than right. Women use both hemispheres for many activities.
Use It or Lose It	**Left** hemisphere shrinks noticeably with age, likely causing irritability and other personality changes.	**Left** hemisphere shrinks minimally with age. Likely to lose tissue in areas concerning memory and viso-spatial, which can cause difficulty remembering and navigating. Temporarily shrinks with pregnancy.
Corpus Callosum (*the "switchgear"—* connects the hemispheres)	Less dense (fewer neurons relative to brain size); shrinks by another 20 percent by age fifty.	Twenty-three percent thicker (more neurons) relative to brain size; does not shrink with age.
Hypothalamus (*the "thermostat"*)	Operates on principle of negative feedback to maintain constancy in emotion.	Operates on principle of positive feedback, which increases emotional highs and lows.

Raging Hormones	**Testosterone** encourages aggression, self-reliance, and the need for sex.	**Estrogen** encourages contentment, heightened senses, and memory. **Progesterone** encourages nurturing.
Chemical Cocktails	**Oxytocin** (trust hormone) appears in lower levels than in women. **Serotonin** (calming chemical) appears in lower levels than women, which makes men more impulsive and action oriented.	**Oxytocin** (trust hormone) appears in higher levels than in men, especially during breast-feeding and childbirth. **Serotonin** (calming chemical) appears in higher levels than in men, which makes women more likely to try to talk their way out of a problem than to take bold action.
Think of this brain as	**A file cabinet:** highly compartmentalized, contained, efficient, and focused. Ability to turn off; 70 percent less activity during rest.	**A large table:** every file is spread out and touches the others. Always active; only 10 percent less activity during rest.

Is a business book an appropriate place to discuss raging hormones? Absolutely. The knowledge of the differences in architecture and the chemicals that fuel our brains arm us with a new interpretation of how men and women naturally vary in their perceptions and actions as consumers.

Testosterone is associated with aggression, competition, self-reliance, self-confidence, and sexual urges. Men have twenty times more testosterone than women and experience six to seven testosterone peaks during each day. In the morning, when testosterone surges are strongest, men are most alert, competitive, and creative, and they perform higher overall on math and spatial tests. Their writing and verbal skills are better later in the day as testosterone levels fall by as much as 25 percent. If you want to close the deal or negotiate next year's contract with a man, schedule meetings in the late afternoon or early evening when he is least aggressive.[9]

Estrogen and progesterone levels change on a monthly cycle from the time a woman reaches puberty until the completion of menopause. Estrogen is credited with making the brain more alert, heightening the senses, increasing absorption of information, and general feelings of contentment. Progesterone releases nurturing feelings and has a calming effect on the brain. Expect that closing the sale with a woman may take more time as she sorts through all of the ways this purchase will affect her life or business.

As hormones decrease with age, men and women become more alike. Perhaps this is why most couples who survive past their fortieth anniversary seem so content with each other. Starting at the age of forty, a man's testosterone level decreases 1 percent each year. This explains why men become more laid-back with age. Many new grandfathers astound their adult children, who hardly recognize the attentive man, so unlike the absentee, workaholic father that raised them. Decreasing testosterone levels, rather than recognition of what they missed the first time around, usually account for the more nurturing behavior. Think you can sell to a retired man the same as you would that executive in his forties? Think again. The retired man might scold you for the same hard-line approach you used successfully last week on the younger VP of marketing.

While men become more nurturing with age, women frequently report becoming more focused, energetic, and self-confident as the decreased estrogen levels reveal their natural testosterone levels. At the completion of menopause, a woman's estrogen level plummets to one-tenth of its earlier level—so low that a man, at any age, will produce higher estrogen levels than a postmenopausal woman. This bears out in statistics that show an increasing percentage of women over fifty-five entering the labor force while workforce participation rates for men in the same age bracket are declining.[10] When selling to a female empty nester, bear in mind that you might want to be quicker to the point than you were with the inquisitive new mom last month. With lower levels of estrogen, your postmenopausal prospect may appreciate a more direct, bottom-line approach.

Chemical Cocktails Served Here

During every waking moment we are bombarded with sensory input, and our brains respond with doses of hormones, blended especially for the occasion and for each gender. As you prepare to market or sell to X and/or Y, you must consider the cocktails by which each is influenced.

Oxytocin is the hormone of trust. Often called the "cuddle hormone," it eases the fear of close contact and betrayal.

The female brain always secretes more oxytocin than the male brain, but during labor, childbirth, and breast-feeding, levels soar. Studies have shown that if oxytocin is inhaled through the nostrils, both men and women become more trusting and will invest more money than those who received a placebo nasal mist. Forget the dreams of piping oxytocin through the HVAC of your brokerage office, showroom, or department store; it only works in a nasal spray form. But there is another way of increasing oxytocin levels—through human touch. Studies show that a fifteen-minute massage causes elevated oxytocin levels. Short of hiring a masseuse to give neck massages in your waiting room, you can increase connection, and eventually trust, by reaching out and touching your client on the arm. Obviously, the timing and circumstances should be appropriate for this; if they are, a benign touch could close the trust gap significantly.

Serotonin soothes the soul and calms the mind. Men have less serotonin than women. This is why a man is more likely to exhibit impulsive behavior during a heated negotiation—slamming his fist down or abruptly leaving the room. With higher levels of serotonin, women are more likely to attempt to talk their way out of a stressful situation before they have to do anything drastic.

Understanding your male and female prospects and customers is empowering. You'll be empathetic to what motivates their decisions—their innate processes—to arrive at a conclusion and the way they want you to communicate with them. These skills will not only give you the ability to sell more goods and services but to be a better friend and partner to both genders. To delve more deeply into gender differences, read on.

2

BUYOSCIENCE

In Search of the X and Y Buy Buttons

Sam was in his early thirties, bright, good-looking, and one of the most tenacious and successful salespeople at his company. But on the day I met him, Sam was mad. He and his sales team had worked for over a year trying to win the networking business of a Fortune 100 company. "I just don't get it," Sam vented to me. "We knew this company inside out. We researched all their options. We nailed the presentation. We had this brilliant PowerPoint with charts that showed how our applications would save the company millions of dollars. And then they choose our competitor, who doesn't have our capabilities or reputation for great service. *What were they thinking?*"

What if you had the power to answer that question? Just ponder that for a moment—what if you could peek inside the heads of your customers, your prospects, your employees, your spouse, and—heaven forbid—even your teenager? What if you could peer inside their minds to answer perhaps the most perplexing question of all: what on earth are they *thinking*?

Well, you can.

As a marketer or salesperson, you are constantly asking your prospect to choose: to choose to notice your product, to choose to grant you time on his or her calendar, to choose to divulge critical information, to choose to buy, to choose to go from being a onetime buyer to a loyal repeat customer and then to choose to refer your services to your next customer. So whether you're the guy who writes the ad copy or the gal who presents the $17.5 million solution to the CEO, by understanding the brain's decision-making process, you can know with a good degree of certainty what your prospect or client is thinking.

BRAIN SCIENCE FOR DUMMIES

In the 1970s and '80s, Pepsi ran blind taste tests, asking people to choose between Pepsi and Coke in what became one of the most remembered TV ad campaigns, the "Pepsi Challenge." Pepsi beat Coke hands down.

Then why does Coke continue to outsell Pepsi twenty-five years later? That's the question Read Montague, a neuroscientist at Baylor College of Medicine, wanted to answer in 2003. Montague reenacted the Pepsi challenge with a couple of twists. First, he watched his subjects' brain activity with an fMRI (functional Magnetic Resonance Imaging), which measures the flow of the blood as it transports glucose—the brain's fuel—to their brains. Not knowing if they had tasted Pepsi or Coke, about half said that they preferred Pepsi. During the second test, Montague told the participants that they were drinking Coke or Pepsi, and three-fourths of them said that Coke tasted better. And with their different choice, there was different brain activity. Coke "lit up" the medial front cortex—a part of the brain that controls higher thinking.[1]

Montague reasoned that when told the drink was Coke, the participants recalled images and thoughts from commercials—and Coke's brand trumpeted taste. So does the human brain provide a rational explanation of why people make seemingly irrational decisions?

This book is about the differences in the male and female brain and how understanding those differences is crucial to your sales success. But before we dive deep into gender nuances, let's take a peek inside the brain to comprehend its function. Once you understand this, the differences will be easy to remember.

Weighing in at about three pounds, your brain makes up less than 2 percent of your total body weight. But it burns 20 percent of your calories. That being the case, scientists' biggest breakthrough is yet to come: how to sit on your behind all day, eat chocolates, and still lose weight.

Your brain comes equipped with one hundred billion neurons, or nerve cells. You have more neurons in this small area than there are stars in the universe. These neurons are standing at attention in a hyperactive state to take in new information. If your brain determines something is important, it calls on your one hundred trillion synapses—specialized junctions that connect the neurons. Think of the first telephone operators manually plugging in a wire to connect callers; that's what your synapses do. This connection makes the neurons fire together and then wire together. And that's what makes a memory.

Your brain is an intricate memory system of connections based on your individual experiences. And intelligence is actually the ability to predict the future by an analogy to the past. Say your cell phone rings. From past experience you know someone is trying to reach you. You look at caller ID and see that it is your mother-in-law. You predict this will be a very long conversation.

Although on any given day you may argue this point, all humans have won the brain lottery. Each one of us has not one but three brains—one stacked on top of another.

THE REPTILIAN BRAIN

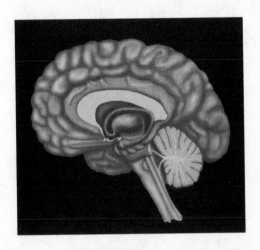

According to Paul MacLean's triune brain theory, buried deep in the back of your skull lies your primitive brain. It is also called the *reptilian brain* because snakes and lizards only have this portion of the brain. But primitive does not mean unimportant. Actually your reptilian brain is very important because it is concerned solely with your survival. It controls your heartbeat, and it makes sure that you take your next breath. It is also responsible for hunger, fear, and sexual attraction, and it determines if you attack or run when in danger. Your reptilian brain filters every stimulus with these three questions: (1) Is it dangerous? (2) Can I eat it? (3) Can I procreate with it? And if the answer is no, your primitive brain is not interested.

THE MAMMALIAN BRAIN

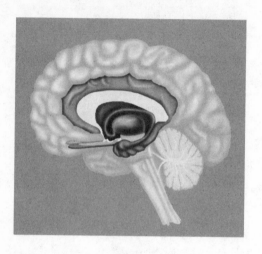

The second brain is one we share with animals, called the *mammalian brain*. It is also called the *limbic system* because it looks like a limb hanging over your reptile brain. The limbic system handles complex emotions such as love, hate, compassion, envy, hope, and contempt. Anyone with a dog knows that mammals are certainly emotionally endowed. Our mammalian brain expresses itself strictly in feelings. When you talk about reaching someone's heart or having a bad feeling in your gut, you are talking about your mammalian brain. It scans the world with one main question: how does this make me feel? A stimulus must evoke feelings for your limbic system to spring to action.

THE EXECUTIVE BRAIN

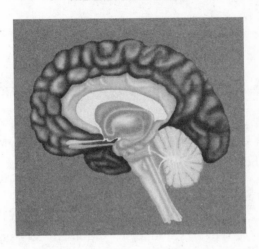

The third brain is the neocortex (literally, "new" cortex)—also called the *executive brain*. It is what makes us human. Resting over the limbic system, the executive brain is where all abstract reasoning, long-term planning, and the processing of words, symbols, facts, logic, and cause-and-effect takes place. The executive brain filters the world rationally.

Once your reptilian and mammalian brains have discarded information as not important—i.e., it's not going to hurt me, I can't eat it, it won't help me produce offspring, and it doesn't make me feel anything significant—your executive brain deals with the leftovers. This is not the part of the brain to which you want to have to appeal. The executive brain is a very tough sell. Unfortunately, most sales and marketing efforts are launched and sunk in the realm of the rigorous executive brain.

APPEALING TO YOUR CUSTOMERS' EMOTIONS

Maya Angelou wisely asserted, "They will forget what you said. They will forget what you did. But they never will forget how you made them feel." If most of your ad campaigns, sales presentations, or prospecting conversations present facts, figures, and logical arguments in a painstakingly prepared PowerPoint presentation, I have some bad news: you and your product are highly forgettable. Whether male or female, your audience's logical, executive brain is hard to arouse—and you don't want to stake your success in that realm of people's brains.

There are two simple reasons why it is hard to capture the executive brain's attention: (1) the reptilian brain, and (2) the mammalian brain. Our brains are wired to tend to the act of *surviving* first (the reptilian brain's function) and to tend to the act of *thriving* second (the mammalian brain's domain). Processing facts, figures, and logic and then using temperance is tedious work. Our brains must first deal with surviving and thriving before we can get our heads around the heady stuff.

Imagine for a minute that you are back in third grade, learning your multiplication tables. For months your teacher flashed those cards: 7x6, 7x7, 7x8. And then finally one day you got the whole sequence right. Then the teacher asked, "What is 8x7?" and you replied with, "Huh?"

This teaching technique is called *spaced and repetitive learning*. Teachers often resort to it when there is nothing captivating about a topic, nothing that can truly arouse our reptilian or mammalian interests. Using spaced and repetitive learning as your only technique can be tedious work.

Now take a hard look at your advertising campaign, your public relations plan, and your next big sales presentation. Are you trying to grab your prospect's attention or close the big sales with numbers, new arguments, and nifty charts? Are you coming across like multiplication tables— using spaced and repetitive messaging, hoping that if they hear your name and product over and over again, they'll finally remember you? Use that strategy, and in the end you'll be no more memorable than ink on a card.

The rest of the chapters in this book will explain the nuances of connecting to men and bonding with women by appealing to emotions. But first, now that we have explored how men and women are similar in processing decisions, let's look at how they are different. In most cases, very different.

Finding a Solution

Prior to 1992, I drove Volkswagens. My beat-up 1968 VW Bug got me through college and graduate school, and my first new car was a white VW Cabriolet. Eight years into the workforce, I decided it was time for my first "grown-up" car.

Intimidated by the thought of analyzing the engine and being swindled by a car salesman, I recruited my husband, Phil, to shop with me. When we arrived at the BMW dealership, I explained to Peter, the salesman, that *I* would be purchasing the car. I then explained I wanted a comfortable commute, and the car needed to be roomy and luxurious enough to chauffeur out-of-town clients when necessary.

Peter and Phil immediately popped the hood of a beautiful, navy blue 325i and expounded on the glories of horsepower, torque, and cylinders. Phil's engineer mind loved the superior design of the BMW engine.

Bored out of my mind, I pulled open the driver's door and inspected the interior. The tan leather was rich and soft, the wood grain glistened on the dash, and I imagined James Taylor serenading me over the Bose stereo system each evening as I drove home.

During the test drive the BMW handled impeccably. It was actually fun to drive. Phil turned to me and exclaimed, "We could drive this car on the Autobahn!" I smiled and thought, *I'm sure we'll be doing that frequently.*

We returned to the dealership, and Phil and Peter began seriously negotiating. Before things went too far, I interrupted their fun. "Peter," I said, "where is the cup holder?"

Peter answered with an indignant tone, "The BMW is the ultimate driving machine. It is not a restaurant."

"Well, I have a forty-minute commute each morning, and I want to drink my coffee on the way."

Peter turned and headed into his office and then returned with a blue plastic cup holder that he hung from the base of the window on the driver's side door panel. "If you must," he cracked, "there is your cup holder."

After envisioning the puddles of coffee and Diet Coke that would frequent my lap over the life of owning this car, I said to Phil, "Come on; let's go to the Lexus dealership." Soon thereafter, I purchased a Lexus . . . with two built-in cup holders, thank you very much. Then for the next ten years, Phil referred to my car as "the $30,000 cup holder."

Men Prioritize and Analyze

The hunter's focused existence prepared modern men to have keen abilities to concentrate on a single goal. When making a purchase, men prioritize options and then analyze features.

Men easily tune out details and outside stimuli that they do not see as pertinent to the buying decision. They channel their thinking and activity to reach a solution, preferably in their own quiet space with a Do Not Disturb sign in place. Remember, the man's brain is a file cabinet: he pulls the pertinent file, sorts through it in his mind, and then solves the problem. Dr. Helen Fisher, of Rutgers University, calls this "step thinking."[2] As my BMW story clearly demonstrates, this is not how women make a decision.

Women Maximize and Synthesize

Throughout history a woman's job description required simultaneous duties, and modern women have inherited a brain that not only is built for multiprocessing, but *prefers* it.

Women make purchasing decisions by including all of the ways the product will affect her life and then synthesizing that information to find the perfect solution. If a man's brain is like a file cabinet, remember that a woman's is like a big table. She looks out across the array of information stacked on that great worktable brain of hers and synthesizes the effect of this product on the many files of her life. Dr. Fisher refers to this as "web thinking."[3]

During our trip to the BMW dealer, Phil singularly focused on the driving experience. I, however, thought about all of the other experiences I would encounter while driving. That is precisely why even the ultimate driving machine would not meet my commuting needs without a built-in cup holder.

DECISIONS, DECISIONS

	Male	Female
Style	Thinks independently, preferably in a quiet spot, then provides solution.	Thinks out loud, brainstorms all possibilities, seeks others' input.
	Thinks in linear steps, eliminates perceived nonessential information.	Thinks in webs, gathers and connects more data, and synthesizes the product's effect on all aspects of life.
Listen for	The top two or three priorities.	The many ways this decision will impact her life and nest.
Focus on	His main concerns.	If you cannot fully alleviate all of her concerns, fully address all objections. Overcome all that can be mitigated. Be honest about those you cannot, and provide a solution to minimize the negative effects. Never dismiss an objection as trivial. Women scorn dismissal.
Pros	He will get to his points and take action if his objections are adequately addressed.	She will tell you how she'll specifically use your product. She may identify benefits that you never dreamed of.
Cons	He may not share all of his objections.	Her sales cycle may be longer because of all of the parts of her life your product will impact.

TAKING SCIENCE TO THE STREET

X: To convince a woman to buy, brainstorm aloud with her. Be flexible and willing to consider all possible ways in which the product will affect her life. She will often tell you the benefits she perceives, and it is those to which you can speak. She will also voice concerns, and you must address those honestly. If she mentions concerns you cannot legitimately alleviate, offer solutions to ease the negative effects. Whatever you do, do not dismiss a single concern. Write one off, and she'll likely write you off. And whenever possible, get her network involved in the decision-making process. Her decision is not as clear-cut as her male counterpart's. She is considering the whole of her experience and how your product or service will make it better, easier, or more beautiful.

Y: To convince a man to buy, you must speak directly to his top priorities. While there are various strategies for trying to manipulate this information from your male prospects, you'd be better off to just ask, "What are your top three priorities?" Then listen to what he says, and adjust your presentation accordingly. To address his objections effectively, don't talk up no-priority features and benefits. He won't care about them, and they won't close the deal. Mentioning them may even kill the deal altogether. It says to him, "You're not speaking my language." Once you've effectively made your case with him, give him some space to think and come to a conclusion. This doesn't tangibly apply if you're *marketing* to the male half, since you're not physically in his presence, but if you're in a *selling* situation and sitting in an office or boardroom, step out for a few minutes. Or perhaps even better, offer him a neutral place to just sit, think, and conclude. Perhaps every sales office that caters, at least in part, to a male customer base should have a safe, masculine-decorated decision room with drinks and a nice view.

3

DIVERSE DRIVES

It's about his quest and her nest.

In the mid 1990s, Cadillac recognized that women were buying luxury cars. To capture this emerging market, they launched an advertising campaign during the 1996 Super Bowl. Figuring what works for him must work for her, they modified the hero's quest story. The ad began, "Once upon a time there was a princess . . . ," as Cindy Crawford, decked out in black leather, cruised across the screen in the new Cadillac Catera.

What were the creators of this campaign thinking? They believed that the ad would appeal to women through "fantasy empowerment." The ad probably appealed to men's fantasies more than women's. But the bottom line was that it didn't sell cars.

In chapter 2 we learned that while our brains are designed to help us predict the future by what we have learned in the past, men use *step* thinking and women use *web* thinking to arrive at a solution. In this chapter we'll explore motivation—what drives men, what drives women—and how understanding these diverse drives can boost your profitability and accelerate the decision-making process for both X and Y.

Here are the overarching motives to bear in mind as we move through this chapter.

- Buying is all about his quest.
- Buying is all about her nest.
- Men value and are thus motivated by respect.
- Women value and are thus motivated by self-esteem.
- He craves risk.
- She calculates risk.

IT'S ALL ABOUT HIS QUEST

Men are drawn to advertising, products, and solutions that tell the traditional hero's story—an independent man with a precision tool overcomes the challenge and makes the world a better place. That tool can be a performance car, credit card, financial plan, power drill, software program, business solution, or job. Throughout history men have conquered new frontiers. Their challenge, purpose, and glory have always been focused out in the world or—most recently—in space. Self-worth comes from conquering the environment in which they live.

The BMW 6 Series ad campaign speaks to a man's mammalian brain, the emotional limbic system. It asserts that the ultimate driving machine is the best tool for going out into the world, where his self-worth is validated. The ad features a single man commanding a performance vehicle across a bridge on his quest. Even in the still shot, you can tell that he is moving fast.

"Legend of the road," the ad reads. "Heir to a six-decade tradition of refining luxury, perfecting performance. Commanding style. Unmatched precision. Pure passion. The 6. The ultimate reward."

While it's easy to see how this BMW ad speaks directly to a man's values of independence and power, you can also use this strategxy to connect to your male customers' values during face-to-face sales interactions. Emphasize his ability to conquer the current business challenge by using your product or service as his primary tool. Your appeal is that your offering will allow him to perfect the performance of his department or company.

IT'S ALL ABOUT HER NEST

In their 1996 Super Bowl campaign, Cadillac incorrectly assumed that men and women shared the same motivations when purchasing a luxury car. They believed that independently affluent women most valued independence, conquest, perfection, and a heroine's journey. And they completely missed the mark.

By the time a woman is thirty, she is over the princess fairy tales and is smack-dab in the middle of a life of responsibility. She is no longer dreaming of perfection. In fact, she laughs at the idea that her life could be perfect.

Throughout history women have been most concerned with preparing the next two generations for survival. She had to constantly orchestrate all the resources in her clan to assure their success each day. Our modern-day female can't imagine thirty minutes, let alone an extended journey, during which time no one was dependent on her for survival.

In her career and her personal life, she most values relationships and credits the strength of her networks as her number one reason for success. Women buy products and services that will nurture their relationships and make their lives just a bit easier and more comfortable.

Ten years after Cadillac failed, Toyota hit the bull's-eye. In this ad the car isn't even moving—it's there waiting to meet her needs. Notice the house (her nest) is lovely but certainly not perfect. There's a foam airplane on the roof, toys strewn across the yard, and she'll probably have to move bicycles out of the driveway before she can leave. But it is real. She can relate to this life. The message is that the Toyota Sienna works for the woman who lives in this home. It therefore motivates a woman who can assert, "My life is like this," to conclude, "The Toyota Sienna is the vehicle for me."

While many minivans are now decked with leather and surround sound stereo systems, no one would classify them as performance vehicles. Yet, with their cup holders, DVD players, and doors that automatically slide shut, they still perform. For the woman who is in the midst of raising children, the minivan is her perfect performance tool.

Perhaps part of Toyota's strategy is banking on the fact that women purchase more than 60 percent of all new cars, not just minivans. It is a major reason Toyota picked up what Cadillac left on the table. Women view cars and other big-ticket products not as the vehicle of their quest for validation but as an integral tool to keep their nests functioning.

Now, let's make this perfectly clear—a woman's nest does not refer solely to her home, family, or children. While she craves success as much as the guy in the next office, your professional female prospect, who is more likely to have multifaceted interests, simply defines power differently. Titles are less important than purpose and contribution. Your female prospect is more interested in influence—over a group of people or her company's future direction—than in independent conquest. She measures success in terms of her team's contribution and will credit her support networks for making it possible. With her, emphasize how your business solution will positively impact her team, making their lives easier and their purpose clear.

RESPECT: HIS VALUE PROPOSITION

Q: What's the only time during a football game that both teams' fans come to their feet to cheer for a single player?

A: When, after lying lifeless on the field, he rises up from a bell-ringing hit and stumbles off the field under his own power.

When men are knocked to the ground—whether literally or figuratively—they view their recovery as more important than the fall. Recovery from a failure is a key element in building respect. Men see failure as a natural learning experience. Whether in determining his own self-worth or respecting the guy or gal in the next office, a man will place a high value on rebounding from failure.

Falling down or looking clueless is often used in beer, shaving cream, and other commercials targeting men. Tide to Go, Proctor and Gamble's instant stain remover, released a thirty-second spot during Super Bowl XLII. The spoof provided a humorous look at the consequences of embarrassing stains, with a "talking stain" overshadowing a man while interviewing for a job. Apply Tide to Go, and the interviewee recovers from his embarrassment and wins the job.

In a sales situation, understand that when a man objects, you have been given an opportunity to shine.

Assertively address and overcome his objection, and you will gain his respect and move much closer to convincing him to buy.

SELF-ESTEEM: HER INTRINSIC CHARGE

Women, on the other hand, value and promote self-esteem. Whereas respect is earned over time through achievement and overcoming failure, women would prefer that everyone feel good about themselves all of the time. While she'll cheer as loud as a man for another's recovery from a fall, a woman doesn't need anyone to fail—and actually prefers that they don't. Joking about others' faux pas works for men but will turn women off.

Can you score big with this seemingly small difference? Absolutely. Dove certainly has with its Campaign for Real Beauty.

Launched by Unilever in 2003 to expand the Dove brand from the tried-and-true Dove soap bar to a wide range of health and beauty products, Dove featured regular women in place of supermodels to celebrate the beauty and self-worth of all women. In addition to capturing the hearts of women, the first series of advertisements received substantial media coverage from talk shows and women's magazines. So much, in fact, that Unilever estimated that the media exposure was worth thirty times more than the paid-for advertising.[1]

Figuring they were onto something, Unilever purchased a thirty-second spot in the commercial break during Super Bowl XL at an estimated cost of two and a half million dollars.[2] And this ad was even more powerful. Why? It wasn't even about women and wrinkles. It did not feature one beauty product. It featured beautiful adolescent girls who worried they were not pretty because of their freckles, their curly hair, their straight hair, their noses, or their skin. And it hit a major nerve with women because they painfully remember the self-consciousness of adolescence, and they want to stop this nonsense of a woman's value diminishing because of such superficial factors. Finally a beauty company was determined to create "a new definition of beauty [that] will free women from self-doubt and encourage them to embrace their real beauty."[3]

In an already crowded beauty products market, TV, print, and poster ads featuring real women with real curves prompted a 600 percent surge for the brand in Great Britain.[4]

HE CRAVES THE RISK

I live in the perfect cul-de-sac for skateboarding. It was not a feature that my husband and I were seeking when we bought the house, but it is apparent from the number of children who come from who-knows-where every Saturday that our little street has just the right slopes and banks to be designated the ultimate natural skateboard park.

It's fun to watch the boys and girls skip over the curb and up their homemade half-pipes and other street obstacles. But a funny thing happens on Saturdays. As the morning passes to afternoon, the stakes get higher. The boys design steeper ramps that the girls think are dangerous, if not suicidal. One day my nine-year-old daughter ran in to tell me that the boys were skating down a neighbor's front porch steps. The girls had all decided that the boys were scripting their own demise and backed away, while the boys' exhilaration rose with the rise in danger.

Whether it's at the skateboard park, exploring a new frontier, or going off to battle for their country, the male gender is fueled by risk. The love of the quest requires men to take great risks, and they are biologically hardwired for perilous situations. Fueled with testosterone, the aggression hormone; greater spinal fluid in the brain, which moves physical impulses from the brain to the body; and less oxytocin and serotonin (calming hormones) than women, men are primed to not only take more risk but to feel exhilarated rather than scared by risk.

Sales and advertising strategies that simulate adventure will rouse a man's interest. And for sales and account management strategies, opt for action activities when entertaining a male client—white-water rafting, skiing, and the ever-popular golf outing will trigger his male hormones to produce a rush.

SHE CALCULATES THE RISK

Women are willing to take risks but are less likely to seek out risky situations just for the sake of living dangerously. Her chemical cocktail of estrogen, progesterone, and higher levels of oxytocin and serotonin have a calming effect that leads her to think (or talk, as we'll see in chapter 7) through challenges rather than take action.

Differences in risk tolerance have obvious implications if you own a travel or adventure company. But what about other businesses and personal services? Merrill Lynch Investment Managers' 2005 survey of one thousand investors—five hundred men and five hundred women —confirmed that men take more risk with money. The survey determined that of those who consider themselves

- "Competitive Investors," 60 percent were male and 40 percent female.
- "Measured Investors," 55 percent were male and 45 percent female.

- "Reluctant Investors," 47 percent were male and 53 percent female.
- "Unprepared," 47 percent were male and 53 percent female.[5]

Products, personal services, and business services with a higher dollar amount usually coincide with a higher implied personal peril in making the purchase. Minimizing this risk for women buyers can help minimize the risk of losing their business.

DIVERSE DRIVES

	Male	Female
Is driven by	His quest.	Her nest.

At work	Values independence, prefers hierarchical structures, defined roles, rules.	Values interdependence, prefers self-directed teams.
Wants	The ultimate performance tool.	The tool that performs.
Values	Self-respect by overcoming difficulty.	Self-esteem through inherent self-worth.
Risk	Stimulates hormones.	Signals the need for careful calculation.
When advertising	Position your product or service as the precision tool for him to conquer his environment.	Position your product as instrumental to making life easier and her nest more harmonious.
When selling	See his objection as your opportunity to prove yourself; emphasize enhanced team performance.	Don't knock the competitor, yours or hers; emphasize enhanced team relationships.

VALUE-DRIVEN SALES

There are definite contrasts in male and female values. Not better or worse values—just different. And these contrasts greatly affect their motives to say yes or no in every buying situation. To sell and market effectively to either gender, you must recognize how the X and Y value systems influence your customers' motivation to completely ignore your offering, purchase your product once, or be married to your brand.

TAKING DIVERSE DRIVES TO THE STREET

X: When positioning your product or service with her, stress the positive impact it will have on those in her network —coworkers, friends, family—as well as in benefits to her individually. Attract her with ads that position your product as the primary tool for making her life easier and her nest more harmonious. Don't knock the competition— hers or yours. She places high value on everyone feeling good about themselves. She is driven by her nest. If you can show her how your offering will enhance her relationships, you will lean her toward buying. If she perceives risk in the buy, you must address it by helping her accurately assess the risk to her liking. In the end, if you can convince her that your offering will allow her to more efficiently and effectively manage her nest, she will be driven to buy.

Y: By emphasizing the value of your product or service as his tool of choice for independence, heightened performance, and overcoming the obstacles in his environment, you will speak to what drives him to buy. If he communicates objections to your offer, treat it as an opportunity to prove yourself worthy of his respect. Falling is okay with him as long as you turn it into a triumph. When it applies, a sure-fire way to do this is to emphasize how your offering will enhance team performance, whether his team is himself and a business partner or himself and an entire company. His drive is all about the conquest. And he is okay if that involves risk, as long as you can convince him of the heroic rewards. Do that and you will move him toward buying.

4

WHAT MAKES HIM TICK, WHAT MAKES HER TOCK

He prioritizes, while she maximizes.

One beautiful Sunday in April, my husband, Phil, spent the entire afternoon organizing the garage. He installed shelves, organized the partially used paint cans and the various bottles of weed killer, and hung the bikes from the ceiling. At 5:15 that evening he announced he was going to Home Depot to get a particular type of bolt that he needed to secure the new wallboard.

I replied with a woman's three favorite words, "On the way . . . ," followed by a list disguised as a question, ". . . will you pick up a quart of milk and drop off the recycling?"

Phil grunted and looked at me as if I had asked him

to donate a kidney. I retorted defensively, "It's on the way. Publix is right next door to Home Depot, and the recycling center is behind the grocery store. Why are you so mad?"

"Because if I pitch the recycling and go to the grocery store, I will not have time to finish my garage project tonight," he replied as he mindlessly chucked the cans and papers in the truck.

This scenario plays out with couples every day. Men become exasperated with their wives when they ask them to complete tasks seemingly unrelated to their singular task. And women don't understand why adding another ten minutes to the overall trip to accomplish two more tasks is such a burden. They are on the way, after all.

In her book *Marketing to Women*, Marti Barletta explains that men *prioritize* their time, and women *maximize* their time.[1] A woman will probably not contemplate running a forty-five-minute errand just to accomplish one task. By adding the recycling and grocery items to Phil's trip to Home Depot, I believed he would have a more efficient trip because I would not have felt productive accomplishing just one task in a trip outside the home. Phil thought otherwise. He was about getting there and getting back to finish his garage project.

There are clearly vast discrepancies in the X and Y definitions of productivity and time management. For sales and marketing professionals, the begging question is, how can knowledge of these discrepancies help you connect to your customers and increase sales?

The hunter's focused existence prepared modern man with keen abilities to concentrate on a single goal. He prioritizes by eliminating minor tasks and then targeting crucial projects. His highly differentiated brain has fewer neurons connecting the two hemispheres (or, as I've stated earlier, it is like a filing cabinet, where tasks are filed separately). Phil's "garage project" file had nothing to do with his family's need to replenish the milk and save the planet from waste.

A gatherer's job description throughout history has required skill in carrying out simultaneous duties, and modern women have thus inherited a brain that is not only built for multitasking but prefers it. A woman's definition of productivity is to maximize the number of activities performed in a period of time. If we had clothes at the dry cleaner's next to Publix, I would have added that to Phil's list as well—four tasks in one trip is better than three. A woman's file system naturally groups and shuffles items to accomplish as many tasks as possible. Filing tasks is really about file sharing. When Phil announces, "I am going out to . . . ," my brain reorganizes all the unrelated tasks that need to be done into the "going-out file," where they are all perfectly related.

A PLACE FOR EVERYTHING

Remember from the first chapter the differences in shopping for a man's versus a woman's suit? A woman will roam all over the store—if not the entire mall—to find her perfect outfit, while the men's suits are always located just inside the main entrance, and organized so that he can get in and out quickly.

Once a man decides on the suit, he moves to the register to pay. In one anchor store at the local mall, Godiva has placed a kiosk stocked with their tempting chocolates directly behind the cash register in the men's department. This display might as well be subliminally whispering, "*Hey, buddy . . . want to be a hero? For only twenty-five bucks you can take me home to your woman. I'm right here. I'm already wrapped. She will love us both.*"

When I present this scenario to a roomful of sales professionals, I ask the men, "Do you buy the chocolates?" With a look of confusion, they say no. When I ask why, the answer is always a resounding, "Because I am there for a suit."

While most men have probably never noticed this kiosk, every woman in the audience knows its exact location. While descending on the escalator, looking down at the men's department to the left, the chocolates beckon, "*We're here. We'll make you happy.*" And even though she came for the perfect suit, seeing the chocolates will remind her of her dear friend Amanda, who loves chocolate . . . and isn't it Amanda's birthday next week? Now this shopping trip is a bigger success—accomplishing not just one but two tasks. She's bought her suit *and* the perfect gift.

How could Godiva get more out of their product placement? For men, a chocolate kiosk in their full view will not trigger a thought to buy if their mission in the mall had nothing to do with chocolates or gifts. Marketing must coordinate with sales. The female salesperson could try to create a benefit for the man to notice and buy the chocolates by saying, "My husband brought home a box of these chocolates for me last week, out of the blue, and it meant so much. Is there anyone in your life that you want to surprise with the perfect gift?" Still, he's there for one reason only, and it's a tough sell to motivate him to add another task. If Godiva wants to sell to men, they'd be better off spending their marketing dollars on getting them to the flagship chocolate store. Or better yet, placing their goodies in a gift store filled with other gifts for women.

Most women will notice the kiosk during their forty-five-second descent on the escalator. An innate gatherer who prefers to make the most of each minute, she will use that forty-five seconds to scan the store for other items that she may need. Make it easy to trigger that need with a sign on top of the kiosk that reads, "Godiva . . . the perfect gift."

MAKING THE MOST OF THE WAIT

> *". . . headed, I fear, toward a most useless place.*
> *The Waiting Place . . . for people just waiting."*
>
> —FROM *OH, THE PLACES YOU'LL GO!* BY DR. SEUSS

A restaurant foyer (as you wait patiently for a table), a doctor's waiting room, or an airport waiting area is not only a "most useless place," but it also produces anxiety for your women customers, who are wired for multitasking. What's a product or service provider to do? If you are wise, you'll let them maximize their time by shopping.

In every Cracker Barrel restaurant, there's a company store filled with music, candy, car-friendly toys to keep the kids busy on the road trip, and a must-have sweatshirt (because who knew it would be this cold in Louisville at dinnertime? It sure was warm in Birmingham when we stopped for lunch).

Cracker Barrel has made waiting for a table highly productive for their female customers, thus boosting their company sales. In 2007, 33 percent of its restaurant customers purchased an item in the company store, accounting for 21.6 percent of Cracker Barrel's total sales.[2] And while women are in the country store shopping, the men are enjoying a checkers game in the rocking chairs on the front porch. Cracker Barrel even turns profits with waiting men. Those famous rockers are the number one item sold at Cracker Barrel, and the jumbo checker/tic-tac-toe set is the sixth most popular item at the savvy restaurant. And you thought they were only concerned with serving tasty, down-home food.

Mike Marolt, a twenty-year veteran of Best Buy, is implementing the Cracker Barrel strategy in hospitals. Convinced that a significant opportunity exists to serve the thousands of patients, families, and employees of large hospitals, his company, eq-life, is joint venturing with large hospital systems to improve hospital campuses with stores equipped with health, wellness, and educational resources, as well as technology products and personal consultants.[3] Under this strategy, whether you're leaving the hospital with a new baby or a new hip, Mr. Marolt wants to make sure you have a convenient opportunity to buy the items you will need once you get home. Hospitals and doctors can increase revenue while increasing patient satisfaction by making these items available on their sites.

In most cases, such a strategy will more greatly benefit and therefore persuade your female customers to buy—and a satisfied wife and mom tends to make a happy home. In this way, there is also an ancillary benefit for the male customers. Either way you look at it, if you want a simple way to boost sales and the effectiveness of your marketing dollars, make use of the time when your customers are waiting. This can apply as much to your storefront business as your online business. The waiting place is a prime place of sales and marketing opportunity.

But proceed wisely in this arena. You must weigh all the implications before promoting multitasking as a sales and marketing strategy, because too many options can decrease sales as quickly as the right additional options increase them.

Always anxious to reduce overhead and labor costs, retailers have added self-checkout lanes, allowing customers to scan their own merchandise. While labor costs have declined, so have sales of snacks, gum, candy, and magazines—those items surrounding the customer in both the traditional and the self-checkout lines. Not surprisingly, women's purchases of these items have sunk the most—50 percent compared to a 28 percent drop for men. It seems there is only so much multitasking a woman can do. When she is busy scanning her items, she has no time to peruse the displays for other purchases. When analyzing the business case for self-checkout, retailers must look at both the customer service implications and the possibility of losing those sales of impulse items at the register.[4]

MAXIMIZING TIME FOR WOMEN

So how do you make the most of your customers' time? For women, determine their most common tasks and adapt your offerings to include at least the top three. Brad Sprigler, owner of Brad Sprigler Designs of Louisville, found that his professional female clients were doing more than just office work in their home offices. "Women multitask, manage home chores and look after their careers at the same time," he explained.

When designing a home office space for Carolyn Chou, a pharmaceutical rep, Brad used furniture that would allow her to concentrate on work while her children, ages five and seven, were also in the room.

"One of the main parts of my office is the window seat," she explained. "It is a workable bench, and underneath are three drawers. Two are for the kids' toys, and one is my stuff." A sofa, TV, DVD, and small refrigerator also allow her to be near her children while she accomplishes her work tasks.[5]

Realizing that women want to maximize their time and space, designer Christopher Lowell is expanding his Office Depot line of furniture to include smaller, movable pieces that focus on appearance and functionality to allow women to work wherever they find the space. He understands, as you should, that a major force for moving women to buy is offering products and services that help them maximize their time with numerous important tasks. Short of spinning out of control, the more tasks women can reasonably fit into a time slot, the better.

PRIORITIZING TIME FOR MEN

What days of the year would you guess that men shoppers outnumber women shoppers? December 22, 23, and 24. Not surprisingly, one in five men had not started their 2007 Christmas shopping as of December 11, according to the Washington DC–based National Retail Federation.[6] This has been a trend since the beginning of retail time and is not likely to ever change.

If you think that men have the Ebenezer Scrooge, "Bah! Humbug!" gene embedded in their DNA, you are wrong. The Christmas, birthday, anniversary, and Valentine's Day spark does not ignite the focused male mind until—well—the date is upon him. Search "Valentine's flowers" on the Web and you'll find more than a million Web sites begging for your order. The florists' sites painstakingly plead to order a week in advance. Valentine's Day is their busiest day of the year. They frequently run out of flowers, especially roses. Many of the Web sites give tips to men to "order flowers and make dinner reservations a week in advance." And their tips to women: "Leave him hints; have his assistant put it on his calendar a week before; team up with a friend: you help her spouse remember while she helps yours." My favorite tip is "Send him flowers a week before Valentine's Day with a note saying how much you are looking forward to a romantic Valentine's weekend."

And do these Internet tips increase sales for florists? Not a chance. Since men buy 73 percent of the flowers for Valentine's Day, florists are wasting their time with these pleas.[7] In a national survey commissioned by the Society of American Florists, only a third of men said that they purchase gifts or make arrangements a week or more in advance. On the other end of the spectrum, 30 percent wait until Valentine's Day or the day before to order or purchase gifts for their sweethearts.[8]

Compare men's habits to women's behavior. While browsing in July, a woman will buy that perfect Christmas gift for her brother. After crossing that task off the always-open gift list in her mind, her only challenge now is to remember where she squirrels the gift away for the next five months.

When surveyed, 69 percent of men said that they were most likely to shop only when they needed a specific item, and 31 percent answered that they enjoyed shopping even just to browse—58 percent of women, on the other hand, enjoy browsing with no specific item in mind.[9]

When a male prospect calls you, he has an issue that needs attention now. And one of their first questions is price. Women are much likelier to have a longer time frame for their decision and will consider many variables in addition to price.

The point of all this: stop fighting Mother Nature. Instead of trying to get men to use their time the way women do, become man's best friend by developing service options that trigger his calendar and provide ideas that will allow him to automatically order gifts as well as other items that he purchases at the last minute.

TIMING IS EVERYTHING

	Male	Female
Time Management	He's singular-task and goal focused.	She multitasks with simultaneous and often noncomplementary goals.
Task Management	He'll prioritize and eliminate tasks of less importance to get the main thing done.	She'll maximize the number of tasks completed in a period.

When completing a purchase	He looks for a specific product in an easy-in, easy-out area.	She searches for the perfect solution, which might be one product or several.
While waiting	He will usually power off to save energy.	Her mind is still searching.

In business, timing is everything. We determine the time to introduce a new product, launch a new advertising campaign, and announce earnings. We strive to shorten the sales cycle, increase impulse purchases, and beat our competitors to market.

To close more business, use your newfound understanding of the X and Y time-use habits to design products, develop services, and introduce options that make men more efficient with their primary singular tasks and women more resourceful with their multitasking.

TAKING TIMING TO THE STREET

X: Women will enjoy a maze of sensory experiences while shopping. Package complementary items in groups with special pricing for the lot of them. When your female customer has to wait, give her an opportunity to continue shopping for complementary items or popular items she might find useful. If she has to wait longer than normal, offer her a "buy one, get one free" coupon. Since she is always searching for the perfect solution to the many roles she—and those in her nest—play, she'll buy a Christmas gift for Aunt June in the middle of August and then use the freebie for herself. To tap into her desire to maximize her time with multiple tasks, trigger her gift-buying needs with suggestive messaging. She'll be grateful for the opportunity to check yet another task off her list.

Y: On the other hand, market and sell to his desire to get in and get out. Gear campaigns and position products to make efficient shopping possible. He won't value the experience of shopping more than the ease of shopping, so instead of trying constantly to up-sell him, build a case for his loyalty. If he has to wait for something, give him an opportunity to relax—this is a far greater value to him than finding something else to buy. If he has to wait longer than normal, make his inefficiency worthwhile for both of you—offer him a notable discount on his next purchase. It tempers his clock-watching and costs you nothing up front, yet could motivate (or remind) him to return next time he's on a mission for a product or service you sell. And about that next purchase, always bear in mind that he won't concentrate on the project, date, or holiday until it is imminent, shopping only when he needs to. Design your store to accommodate his last-minute shopping nature.

5

TARGET THE EYE OF THE BEHOLDER

He sees like a laser;
she sees like a lighthouse.

It's Friday night. Exhausted from our hectic week, my husband, Phil, and I plan to unwind in front of the television. Phil pounces on the remote control, holds it high in the air, and exclaims, "I have the power!"

And the surfing begins. He bounces from a police drama with a high-speed chase to a basketball game to a war movie with body parts flying through the air to two male attorneys arguing on a rerun of *Law and Order*. I sigh, "Finally, a male protagonist that speaks."

After choosing the classic war movie *Full Metal Jacket*, and programming the basketball game in Picture in Picture, Phil proudly declares, "Who says men can't multitask?"

I try to connect to the movie, while struggling to ignore the distraction of the game in the corner. After fifteen minutes I concede defeat, grab my copy of *The Lovely Bones*, and retreat to the bedroom to devour the haunting and heartbreaking story of a fourteen-year-old girl who is raped and murdered. It is every bit as brutal and violent as the battlefield scenes on the TV, but I am completely engaged as Susie keeps watch on her family, friends, and her killer, from heaven. I empathize with the characters as if they lived next door.

My evening with Phil mirrors that of many other women with their husbands. What explains the difference?

Jumping from program to program or simultaneously watching golf and football is actually relaxing to the male brain. Blood flows naturally to his four spatial reasoning centers, which allows him to be entertained without working hard. Because he is innately gifted to focus on movement, a man can actually "zone out" in front of a violent war movie.

Switch the channel to a movie with highly emotional conversation, and he has to wake up just to follow along. Keeping up with the characters, dialogue, and emotions is way too much work for a Friday night. Women, on the other hand, have 15 percent more blood flow to areas processing conversation and emotion. A tearjerker stimulates all of a woman's innate verbal and emotional reasoning skills. But it is work for her to engage in the perpetual motion that he craves.

MEN SEE A THIRD DIMENSION

Navigating and hurling spears through the air at moving targets developed men's keen spatial aptitude—the ability to manipulate objects in space. That skill was fine-tuned over thousands of years and is now hardwired in his brain. When a man contemplates a geometry problem, aims at a moving target, or is called on to see things from a three-dimensional perspective, his brain responds with at least four specific areas on the right hemisphere and two minor areas on the left hemisphere to assist him.[1]

Hardwired for watching objects rotate through space, men have gone to great lengths creating extremely tough and often dangerous games for their enjoyment—think football, basketball, hockey, and soccer. Now that you understand a man's innate passion for action and movement, you can anchor your product or service in his mind.

DIFFERENCE IN BRAIN ACTIVITY DURING SPATIAL REASONING

(The drawings depict brain activity shown by the shading from fMRI studies.)

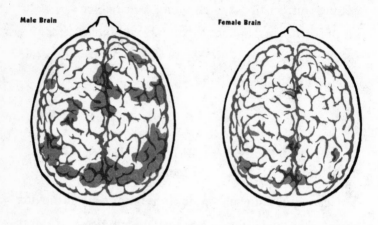

Male Brain   Female Brain

Lawrence H. Summers, the former president of Harvard University, must have been up on this research in 2005 when he suggested that women might not have the same innate abilities in math and science as men. During a NBER (National Bureau of Economic Research) conference in 2005 at Cambridge, he spoke on "Diversifying the Science and Engineering Workforce." He was asked why there were not more women in academia in the hard sciences: math, physics, and engineering. His response provoked a flurry of controversy and later contributed to his resignation. Among other things, he hypothesized that there are differences in the intrinsic abilities of men and women in these subjects (more specifically, men's higher variance in aptitude, abilities, or preferences relevant to science and engineering).

Dr. Summers's statements offended and were vehemently argued—unfairly, in my opinion—for two main reasons:

1. People who disagreed with Dr. Summers pointed to the fact that women are pretty darn good at math. They get better math grades all through school, and more than half of accounting majors are now women.

True. True and true again. But there is one area of math that most men grasp better than most women: spatial reasoning—the ability to manipulate objects in space.

Remember these types of questions on the SAT? Compare the four shapes below to the test object. Which one is the test object rotated? (The answer can be found on page 85.)

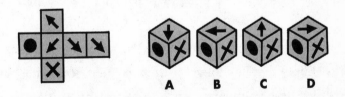

This is the part of math that most men "get" and "get quicker" than most women. Heightened spatial reasoning skills do not enable men to be better at all math skills, but it certainly gives them a leg up on these types of problems. This same innate ability also makes men, on average, better parallel parkers than women. I use map-reading skills when I give seminars to exemplify the difference between the sexes in this arena. A woman will invariably say, "But I love maps."

"So do I," I say, "but if you are navigating in a large, unfamiliar city and you turn right, do you rotate the map to face the direction you are headed?"

Women nod; men look on in disbelief. They never think of rotating a map, because they don't need to. Their spatial skill allows them to swivel the map in their minds.

2. People also disagreed with Dr. Summers because they thought his implication that women may not have the innate abilities that men do was sexist and stereotyping.

It's important to note that Dr. Summers did not imply that he thought a woman could not be the greatest mathematician or scientist of all time. Scientists believe that about 10 percent of women have the heightened spatial aptitude of men. This likely explains why 11.5 percent of all architects, 10.6 percent of all engineers, and less than 3 percent of all air traffic controllers are women. It's not that women can't perform these jobs; some women can and do. But most women would find it much harder to be great at jobs that required superb spatial reasoning skills.

A friendly warning to my readers, and mostly my male readers: women have worked hard to achieve political and economic parity with men and for good reason are sensitive to any suggestion that they cannot perform a certain task or job. Learn from the Dr. Summers debacle. Just because the "math thing" is now clear doesn't mean it is wise to use it to explain certain behaviors. A primary goal of all effective marketing and selling is effective communication with both genders. And sometimes what is helpful to know is not helpful to tell.

MEN ARE EQUIPPED
WITH NATURAL BLINDERS

"Honey, will you change the lightbulb in the kitchen ceiling light?" she asks.

"Sure, where are the lightbulbs?" he replies.

"In the pantry," she replies, thinking to herself, *the same place they have been for the last seven years.*

Standing in the pantry, looking at the shelves, he says, "I don't see them."

"They're on the third shelf on the right."

"We must be out of lightbulbs. I don't see them."

She walks into the pantry, turns to the right, pulls a lightbulb out of its box, and hands it silently to her husband.

Later, my friend Nancy recounted this encounter between her and her husband, Mark, while we were at lunch. She was convinced that Mark was playing helpless so that he wouldn't have to change the lightbulb. She was incredulous when I suggested that maybe he really didn't remember where the lightbulbs are stored, and he really didn't see them.

The hunter needed vision that could zero in on moving targets at a distance. To completely focus on a target, the male brain can tune out the unimportant objects in the periphery, making it hard to spot a stationary object outside his tunnel.

Your company may develop and launch the coolest tool ever for men, but if you don't place it in his line of sight as he walks into the store or enters your Web site, he may never find it. His eyes do not naturally search. He prefers to know his precise target and focuses his eyes on hitting the bull's-eye. To effectively market and sell to him, position your products in the center of his focus.

EYES IN THE BACK OF HER HEAD

Turns out that the old saying "Mom has eyes in the back of her head" is more of a slight stretch than a gross exaggeration. With an arc of at least 45 degrees on each side as well as above and below her head, women have wider peripheral vision than men.[2]

The gatherer had to remember the bush that produced berries last summer and then scan through the brush to find it again year after year. Subsequently the female brain has developed a keen system to remember objects and their locations. While he can see a specific target farther in the distance, she is blessed with the ability to notice all that is going on around her.

Savvy retailers capitalize on women's innate ability to see it all by placing the staple items in the corners of the store. Browse through any Wal-Mart, and you'll find the disposable diapers located in the back corner of the baby department. Sleep-deprived mothers are wired to gather the "nice-to-have" items on their way to picking up the staples—formula and diapers.

Whether you are a retailer or provide a service, when targeting women, think about what other services or products she must have. Position your offering in such a way that she will see it while she is searching—and she is always searching—on the way to buy her staple item.

THE EYE OF THE BEHOLDER

Not only are male and female brains wired differently; the sexes don't share the same eye structure. All images form in the retina, which converts light into a neurological signal to the brain. The retina is made up of cells called *rods* and *cones*. Rods are color blind—seeing only black and white—while cones are sensitive to color.

Rods and cones send their signals to the two types of ganglion cells: magnocellular (M cells) and parvocellular (P cells).

The M cells and P cells have very different jobs. The M cells, which are primarily wired to the rods, serve as the brain's motion detectors. P cells send information to a particular region of the brain that appears to specialize in analyzing texture and color. And guess what? Men's retinas have more motion-detecting M cells than texture- and color-analyzing P cells; while women have more P cells than M cells.

This difference explains not only the disparity in the perception of motion but in color. Naturally endowed with an abundance of color-sensitive P cells, women are more sensitive to all colors and shades, but especially to red, orange, green, and beige. Men and their M cells prefer black, blue, gray, and silver.[3]

When designing products and packaging, remember that men and women may see an item differently. Use focus groups to confirm that your male and female audiences perceive the product the way you intend for them to see it.

APPEAL TO MEN WITH OBJECTS, GADGETS, AND MOTION

Want to make a man's brain literally light up? Create messages and images in his direct line of vision that include action, show movement, or include gadgets. The structural differences in a man's brain account for his innate reaction when he sees an object: *Where is it? Where is it going? How fast is it moving?*

When promoting products to men, place them directly in their line of vision and make the product move. Rotating your product in space is male brain candy. Since you will have a hard time getting his attention with words alone, you must be particularly creative when marketing services. Link your service in his mind to action and movement. Sponsoring sports events and highlighting the positive momentum will often pique his interest.

Not surprisingly, one particular moving object has a heightened effect on the male brain—a woman. His naturally high testosterone levels combined with his fascination with moving shapes make the sight of a moving woman irresistible. This certainly has not been lost on beer advertisers.

Women often complain that men initially see women as objects. They are probably right but should not be offended. Scientists have concluded that two-day-old boys prefer to watch mobiles while infant girls prefer the human face. Men and women are wired to find different things fascinating. If you're a marketer, recognizing this fact will help you appropriately position products. If you're a salesperson, this should help you empathize with the opposite sex.

FOR HER, SEEING IS RELATING

While his brain is processing, *Where is it? Where is it going? How fast is it moving?* her brain ponders, *What's that, and how does it relate to me?*

If the lightbulb he initially did not see suddenly fell off the pantry shelf, Mark would most likely catch it. Nancy, on the other hand, would likely scream and wonder why a lightbulb would attack her.

While men are mesmerized by motion, women are engrossed by emotion.

Objects rotating through space might catch her eye, but she's more likely to duck and cover than reach out for it. To grab a woman's attention, use faces of people to whom she relates. Pictures of women that look like her *with* people that are similar to her network of friends and family—remember, women value interdependence, not independence—will resonate most with her.

HE SEES . . . AND WANTS TO KNOW
HOW IT WORKS

A man's heightened spatial reasoning also gives him an advantage with mechanics. When he buys a car, electronics, or a lawn mower, he will want to understand how it works. With a man, be prepared to discuss the features of your product, detailing the working mechanisms and any installation or ongoing maintenance that he might want to do himself.

Deep inside every man is the boy who loves to tinker

with mechanical gizmos. A few years ago Forbes featured a "make your own helicopter kit" as one of its executive toys. For a mere $69,000, a company would ship all the parts of a helicopter with assembly directions. Clearly marketed to male executives, the ad warned that you might as well go ahead and get a divorce prior to ordering the helicopter, because the project would take every minute of your spare time for the next eighteen months. Many guys were drooling to take on the challenge, then watch the copter take flight.

Not only is superior engineering and mechanics the key selling feature for products like drills, that are predominantly bought by men; products that are traditionally bought by women can find their own profitable niche by also enticing men through superior engineering. If you don't believe me, take a look at Dyson and their vacuum cleaners.

Who would have ever thought that men would be interested in the tedious chore of vacuuming the floor? Well, truth be told, they aren't. But since Jim Dyson opened his first factory in 1993, men have been interested in the vacuum cleaner. Men's interest in this superior tool and its cool mechanics has fueled Dyson's sales to over $6 billion worldwide.[4]

Even though most vacuum cleaners are used by women, there is nothing feminine about the Dyson. It is clearly marketed to men. The only person featured on its Web site is Jim Dyson. What's more, there is a whole section offering cool games that appeal to men's innate spatial acuity.

Dyson has risen to the top of its industry by appealing not only to the primary end user—a woman—but also to a man. The novel way the vacuum works and its superior design captured the male mind. So great was the allure that men actually created the buzz around Dyson. Believe me, when a man suggests buying a new vacuum cleaner and paying a premium for superior design and performance, it gives a woman just enough hope that he also might want to operate the vacuum cleaner. You will not find her arguing but instead burning up the road between her home and the nearest Target for a Dyson. I should know—it is precisely what happened in my household.

SHE JUST WANTS IT TO WORK

While I was writing this chapter, I received this cry for help through an e-mail from a woman who belongs to Cable, a network of about five hundred professional women in Nashville:

Re: Home electronics—HELP!
CABLE friends,
    I have a plethora of home electronics gear that

isn't working together. I know it is possible for the flat screen TV, DVD player, CD player, VCR, receiver, and miscellaneous speakers to all work, but can't seem to figure out how to make that happen.

I am in desperate need of someone to come into my home, hook all this stuff up, and show me how to use it (there must be fifteen remotes!) for less than a mortgage payment. I have a smokin' new workout DVD that I can't use, and really need to.

Can someone recommend this person?

Thanks!

Lynn

Your female customer just wants to know that the vacuum cleaner, home electronics, or car she is purchasing will work. She needs assurance that it will require little or no work on her part to install, operate, and maintain it. Yes, there are some women who may be interested in torque, RPMs, and the benefits of the engine design, but most aren't. When your customer is female, it is best to ask if she wants an explanation of the technical components of your product. Launching into a lengthy diatribe of techie features may make her eyes roll back in her head.

To test gender differences in mechanical aptitude, researchers at Yale gave college students the written instructions for programming a VCR. Sixty-eight percent of men conquered the task on the first try. Only 16 percent of the women were successful on the first pass.[5]

To win with women, drop the in-depth commentary on superior engineering. Instead, assure her that your product or service is reliable—and that it will work when she needs it. Also offer installation and service plans that make purchasing and maintaining the product much easier.

SEEING IS BELIEVING

	Male	Female
The Lights Are On	In four specific areas on the right hemisphere, and in two minor areas on the left hemisphere.	In one diffuse area on the right, and one diffuse area on the left.
Traits	Higher geometry aptitude.	Lower geometry aptitude.
	Better at navigation.	Turns maps to navigate.
	Solves math problems nonverbally.	Talks through a math problem.
	Prefers left eye when performing spatial functions.	Uses both eyes when performing spatial functions.
Stark Differences	Better at parallel parking.	Longer time to parallel park.
	68 percent of men can program a VCR on the first try.	16 percent of women can program a VCR on the first try.
	Sees an object and thinks, *Where is it, where is it going, and how fast is it moving?*	Sees an object and thinks, *What is it, and how does it relate to me?*
Vision	Tunnel vision (narrow range) with better depth and perspective.	Wide peripheral vision; takes it all in.
	Prefers black, blue, gray, and silver.	Sees wider range of colors and shades.
	Visualizes third dimension.	Better visual memory.

	Better vision in bright light.	Better night vision.
	Think of it as a laser beam.	Think of it as a lighthouse.

Armed with the vision of how to target the eye of your beholder, you can use these innate gender preferences to ignite your customers' interest. By incorporating the remaining four senses that you'll learn about in the next chapter, you'll be able to arouse emotion to connect your brand to X and Y.

TAKING VISION SMARTS TO THE STREET

X: Women are drawn to the human face. They prefer texture and richness of color. When creating an ad to grab the attention of X, employ rich reds, oranges, greens, and beiges in particular. Women are most sensitive to these hues. Throw in some texture and women won't be able to turn away. When selling to a woman, spend time assuring her that your product or service works. Demonstrate if appropriate, and always offer no-worry installation and service plans that ensure her purchase will make life for her and her nest-mates easier.

Y: Objects moving through space are male brain candy. When positioning your products or ads online or in a store, put them in an obvious line of sight, and then make them move. The Y eye will find them. When selling to men, discuss how your product or service works. Promote superior engineering and mechanics, both captivating topics to the male brain.

(The answer to the spatial reasoning question on page 71 is A.)

SENSE AND SENSIBILITY

He's more sensible, and she's more sensitive.

Imagine it's a damp November morning in 1994, and you are walking down the streets of New York City. A young man hands you a cup of coffee and says, "Would you taste this and tell me what you think?" The warmth of the cup thaws your frozen fingertips as you breathe in the rich aroma of the brew. As the first sip of java travels down your throat, the fog starts to clear from your mind. You smile and tell the market researcher that it really hit the spot.

"Great!" he replies. "In three months we'll have a coffee shop here. How often do you think you'll stop on your way to work and buy a cup for four dollars?"

"Four bucks? You've got to be kidding," you reply and walk on, while your logical executive brain continues to process. *What is he smoking? Four bucks for a cup of coffee when I can get it for free in seven minutes when I reach the company break room?*

Fortunately for Starbucks, their recipe for success doesn't rely on only the executive brain's logical conclusions. Their strategy appeals to all of your senses. They have designed their stores to be your "third place." With the comfort of home and the ability to work undisturbed, Starbucks provides an aesthetically appealing place to either relax or be productive, or relax while being productive. As you unwind to the music in the background, your brain is stimulated by the smell, taste, and feel of the rich, warm espresso. And within seconds of swallowing the brew, you experience a pleasant buzz from the powerful yet legal stimulant—caffeine. The Starbucks experience permeates all of our senses. Thus it is a recipe that trumps common sense every time.

Michael Moe, author of *Finding the Next Starbucks: How to Identify and Invest in the Hot Stocks of Tomorrow*, attributes Starbucks' market cap growth from $220 million in 1992 to $23 billion in July 2007 to his four *P*s of future superstar companies: great *people*, leading *product*, huge *potential*, and *predictability*.[1] I add a fifth *P* to the equation: *permeate*—the ability to reach each of your customers' five senses.

Every new idea, conversation, bump in the road, or blue sky ahead is brought to your brain through your five senses. Then your brain processes the information through patterns so that you can predict outcomes. But as we learned in chapter 2, if the predicted outcome is meaningless, the brain doesn't bother with forming a memory. We are blessed with brains that naturally want to save hard drive space for information and memories that are critical to our survival.

The average adult is now exposed to 294 TV ads per day. Add to this count the astounding number of print ads, obnoxious billboards, and Web site pop-ups that confront you each day, and you can appreciate your brain's screening function. It is such a good screener that a CAB/Nielsen study in April 2000 revealed that as the number of advertising messages soar, ad recall plummets—estimating that only ten to twenty ads produce a fleeting awareness of brand.[2]

While 83 percent of all commercial contact is visual, marketers are now exploring the use of the other four senses to capture their prospects' discerning attention.[3] Now that you understand how men and women see the world differently, let's examine the other four senses and how to target your male and female prospects in a sensory and sensible way.

THE NOSE KNOWS

Read the first scenario below. Close your eyes for at least fifteen seconds and fully imagine the experience. Then repeat while picturing each of the other situations:

1. Your grandmother removing her homemade apple pie from the oven.
2. Popcorn popping in your college dormitory.
3. Walking by a bakery that specializes in artisan breads.
4. Washing your dog after he rolled all over a dead animal.
5. Switching on your heater for the first time of the year.
6. Opening your meat freezer after returning from a vacation to realize that the power had been out for days.

While imagining the popcorn popping, did you remember the buttery aroma luring you away from your studies into your neighbor's room or recollect the time that it popped just thirty seconds too long, and for weeks your dorm room smelled like burnt hair?

Although 83 percent of commercial stimulus comes through your eyes, scent is the most powerful trigger to your emotions. "Seventy-five percent of the emotions we generate on a daily basis are affected by smell," says Martin Lindstrom, coauthor of *Brand Sense: Build Powerful Brands Through Touch, Taste, Smell, Sight, and Sound.* "Next to sight," says Lindstrom, "it's the most important sense we have."[4]

Even if you are trying to recall the past, your nose is a

better guide than your eyes. According to the Sense of Smell Institute, people can recall smells with 65 percent accuracy after a year, while the visual recall of photos sinks to about 50 percent after only three months.[5]

The release of these scientific data has spurred retailers to incorporate scent into their brands. And while you would expect a Bath & Body Works or Ralph Lauren store to have a particular scent, technology retailers Samsung and Sony each have developed their own scent, hoping to attract customers to their stores. These technology companies are hoping that, once there, customers lured in by these alluring scents will linger just a little bit longer or possibly part with $1,500 for a new laptop.

The research smells promising. Xiuping Li, a researcher at the National University of Singapore, found that women in a room with a hidden chocolate chip cookie–scented candle were much likelier to spontaneously buy a sweater than women in a room with a hidden unscented candle (67 percent versus 17 percent).[6]

Vanilla also seems to drive women to the cash register. Dr. Eric Spangenberg, dean of the College of Business and Economics at Washington State University, diffused a subtle smell of vanilla in the women's department of a clothing store. Sales nearly doubled on the days of his study versus the days with no lingering vanilla scent.

Wondering if what was good for the goose is good for

the gander, he set up this exact trial in the men's department of the same Pacific Northwest clothier. The vanilla scent actually kept men's wallets in their pants, as sales declined below average. Knowing that guys actually prefer a whiff of rose maroc, he lightly released this spicy, honeylike fragrance in the shopping area. When he examined the cash-register tapes on the days of the rose maroc infusion, he found an almost 50 percent increase in sales.[7]

Researchers have long known that women are more sensitive to all scents than men. But recently they have also found differences in scent preferences. While men don't notice the smell of Exaltolide (a musklike odor), women are extremely sensitive to the scent. Sandalwood, which is a woody and musky aroma, scores highest on sensuality among U.S. females.

NICE TOUCH

I love my personal financial advisor, Scott. Phil and I have worked with him for over five years with great results. But the relationship started on shaky ground. When first introduced, I held out my hand, and his idea of a firm handshake temporarily paralyzed my right hand while I fought back tears of pain. I wish I could say this is the only time that a well-intentioned man's first greeting triggered pain and subsequently my desire to avoid all future contact with him.

This is not rocket science—most women's hands are smaller and have more delicate bone structure than men's. Coupled with the fact that a woman's skin is at least ten times more sensitive than a man's, and that she may wear a ring on her right hand, it is no wonder that men have the potential to cause excruciating pain with a well-intentioned greeting.[8] To my male readers, I want you to do a little market research today. Find three women you trust, and shake their hands. Ask them to rate your handshake. You want it to be firm but friendly.

And to my female readers, if you meet a man whose handshake is a bit too enthusiastic, let him know. While in Scott's crushing grip, I said, "Whoa, buddy. Your handshake is too strong for me. Let's start over." Once I showed him the temporary ring indentation and explained the pain, he apologized. We shook hands again, and I complimented him on his newfound greeting. He thanked me, and he has seen an increase in female clients.

LEND ME YOUR EAR

From birth, females are more sensitive to sound than males. Multiple studies have found that newborn girls' hearing is substantially more sensitive than newborn baby boys', especially in the 1,000- to 4,000-hertz range, which is important to speech discrimination. This difference only increases as the babies grow into teenagers.[9] And adult women are more sensitive to sound, and especially tone of voice.

Women may need to lower their voice pitch and speak louder than comfortable to be heard well by men. And men need to understand that their voices seem louder—which may sometimes translate to more aggressive—to their female customers.

While women are more sensitive to sound, I would be remiss to not mention the importance of music to both the male and female brains. The brain loves music. In his book *This Is Your Brain on Music: The Science of Human Obsession*, Daniel J. Levin convincingly argues that music is a human obsession, as fundamental to us as language. Music makes it easy for your synapses to "fire together and wire together" to form a memory that might not otherwise be stored. Hence that subversive jingle that you can't get out of your head.

As I write this book, my youngest daughter is in fourth grade. Last month she came running in from the bus and said, "Mom, listen to what we learned today." And to the tune of "Oh My Darling, Clementine," Caroline sang, "Condensaaation, evaporaaation, precipitaaaation on my mind. This is just the wa-ter cy-cle, and it haap-pens all the time."

Now, that is brilliant. Seven years from now, when Caroline is taking the SATs, she may be asked to identify the water cycle. The song she learned in fourth grade will pop into her mind and hopefully connect to all of the other things she has stored about the water cycle. Much of what we learn in school is facts. And the brain thinks facts are boring. Many teachers use the spaced and repetitive learning technique to get kids' brains to store and recall the tedious stuff.

But the enlightened teacher will use brain teasers—music being perhaps the most powerful—to help kids commit a fact to memory. Enlightened marketers must realize that many people hearing their message just don't care about the facts or features of their product. Use music to make your message stick and keep your brand on the tops of your customers' minds.

IT'S A MATTER OF TASTE

By now you have caught on that women are a sensitive sex. Not surprisingly, women have a heightened sensitivity of taste to complement their other keen senses. It makes sense that our female ancestor's job description included tasting the roots and berries to check that they were ripe, sweet, and, especially, not poisonous before gathering them for the clan.

The fact that women prefer sweet and sugar tastes has not been lost on chocolatiers, while makers of beer and snacks target men's taste for salty and bitter flavors. When picking the menu for your next client dinner, offer a variety of entrées, as the kick he gets from the spicy Cajun dish may be too much for her palate. And don't be offended if he douses your favorite tilapia dish with Tabasco. Some—particularly men—like it hot.

THE SIXTH SENSE: INTUITION

"Truly successful decision making relies on the balance of deliberate and instinctive thinking."

—FROM *BLINK* BY MALCOLM GLADWELL

Intuition has received a bad rap in the information age. Often thought of as hocus-pocus, mind-reading, or "that woman's thing," intuition is an immediate recognition or apprehension by the mind, without cognitive reasoning. In business we dismiss it for hard-core facts, reasoning, and analysis. But wouldn't you love to read the minds of your customers, multimillion-dollar prospects, competitors, and investors? Wouldn't it be great if you could shorten the time it takes to make decisions? In some cases you can. Intuition is alive and well and living right below your conscious mind, ready to warn you of danger or lead you to the right answer in seconds.

Frequently we describe intuitive feelings this way:

"That report left a bad taste in my mouth."
"He makes my skin crawl."
"I have a gut feeling; let's go for it."
"I can't put my finger on it, but this just smells rotten."
"It just doesn't sound right."

Everything comes to us through our senses. Then our brains process the information through patterns so that we can predict outcomes. Intuition is that immediate gut feeling (sorry, it's not concrete; you can't manipulate it in a spreadsheet or put it into a clever chart) triggered by something in the environment that your unconscious mind recognizes as important. "Hello," intuition says, "I'm trying to help." Your unconscious mind is trying to tell you something. Sit up and take notes.

OKAY, WELL, MAYBE IT *IS* A WOMAN'S THING

If you are an expert, trading the gut-wrenching rationalizations for your intuitive hunch can save time and headaches. But when it comes to intuitive people-reading, women are experts.

According to Helen Fisher, a Rutgers University professor of anthropology and leading expert in gender differences, women are better at reading tone of voice and body language and are more empathic and intuitive. With the exception of long-distance vision, women's senses are better. These sensitivities add up to excellent "mind-reading" skills. "Women's extraordinary people skills," explained Fisher, "grew from taking care of and responding to babies over hundreds of thousands of years."[10]

In 1997, neuroscientist Davis Skuse of the Institute of Child Health in London found that a gene or cluster of genes on the X chromosome influences the development of the prefrontal cortex, the portion of the brain that controls higher thinking. This gene or gene cluster, silenced in all men and active in 50 percent of women, gives these women a heightened ability to integrate and read social nuances.[11] So what the poet Kipling once asserted is occasionally true after all: "A woman's guess is much more accurate than a man's certainty."[12]

If you are a woman who has great intuitive hunches

and can read a room of people, collectively and individually, trust your gut and speak out. If you are an executive, recognize her talent and involve such a woman in major sales presentations and negotiations. When the rest of the team is thinking, *We are nailing this presentation*, she's the one reading the CFO's "I-don't-buy-this" body language and catching the CIO rolling his or her eyes.

MAKING SENSE OF IT ALL

	Male	Female
Intuition	This DNA is turned off in all men.	Fifty percent of women have turned-on DNA that further heightens their intuitive skills.
Hearing	Right ear preference.	Equal hearing in both ears. Better overall hearing.
Touch	Insensitive skin.	Highly sensitive skin.
	Slower response to pain.	Quicker response to pain.
	Less sensitivity to pain.	Greater sensitivity to pain.
	Less capable of coping with chronic pain.	More capable of coping with chronic pain.

Taste	Likes salty tastes.	Likes sweets and subtle tastes.
Smell	Less sensitive. Rose maroc scent increased sales.	More sensitive to all smells. Vanilla and chocolate chip cookie scents increased sales.

TAKING THE OTHER FOUR SENSES TO THE STREET

X: When women are your target customer, light up that candle, especially if it releases a vanilla or chocolate-chip scent. Women seem to spend more money with those sweet aromas in their nostrils. And speaking of sweet—if you're selling or serving food to female customers, you'd be remiss to not offer some sugary goodies. Their sense of taste craves these more than anything else. In other words, you're not likely to up-sell those bags of pretzels at the register unless they're covered in milk chocolate. Put out a plate of chocolates near your most popular product, and women will stick around longer. And when you close the deal with a woman, don't put a vise grip on her right hand. Her highly sensitive bone structure and skin will tell her to never shake your hand again.

Y: Since men's intuition DNA is turned off, you must appeal directly to their senses when marketing or selling. Their sense of touch is not nearly as heightened as women's, so shake your male customer's hand firmly, without hesitation.

If you play music in your store and you cater only to men, you can turn the volume up on the background music. Men's hearing is not as sensitive as their counterparts', and short of it blaring, they probably won't mind it (though you do need to know what type of music your men customers tend to like). If you're selling food to prospects or serving food to clients, remember that men like it salty and often spicy too. But don't bother trying to win over your male customers with a nice-smelling candle in the back of the store. It won't work unless that candle happens to smell like rose maroc. Otherwise, you're better off to not risk a stockroom fire, since some scents in your store may actually hinder sales.

7

GIVE THEM SOMETHING TO TALK ABOUT

He gives directives; she seeks consensus.

Women concede the parallel parking medal to men but will win the blue ribbon for talking every time. While hunting required silence, the gatherer was in constant communication with the children, the elderly, and the other women back at the camp. The result? Women excel at verbal and written communications. And it shows up in both product preferences and communication styles.

> *Number of words and communication*
> *signals in an average day:*
>
> | MEN | WOMEN |
> |-----|-------|
> | 7,000 | 20,000 |

THE GIFT OF GAB

While women have advanced their verbal skills through thousands of years of regular use, they were also born communicators. While men have more than one specific brain area for spatial activities, women have at least two specific areas for speech and language on *each* side of their brains. This explains why eight women can engage in simultaneous conversations on four different subjects without missing a beat. Men, who do not have multiple areas for speech and language, interpret simultaneous conversations as senseless chatter or crowd noise.

Your female client will consider the business dinner conversation stimulating if it moves from her vacation at the beach last week to her daughter's choice of college to her department's monthly financials to her son's upcoming wedding, which brings the conversation back to her beach vacation because her son will be honeymooning in Hawaii. Your male client likely finds this conversation scatterbrained—even unnecessary—as these topics are not related in his mind and certainly have nothing to do with the business at hand.

All salespeople must build trustworthy relationships with their prospects to become a trusted advisor and not merely a vendor. The first step in this process is establishing a comfortable level of communication between you and your client. Your job is to create that security by adapting to *your clients'* style of communication, not coercing them to adapt to *yours*. With her, move easily through various topics, noting how each relates to her. For him, stay on topic—the product, service, or business at hand—and finish that topic before transitioning to the next. What follows are the major differences in how men and women communicate and how you can market and sell more effectively by communicating in his or her preferred style.

WOMEN WARM TO WORDS, MEN TO PICTURES

The $1.2 billion romance fiction industry accounts for 55 percent of all popular mass-market fiction sold each year. And who's reading all those romance novels? Women. These stories of love are filled with lust, danger, mystery, and violence. Paranormal erotica that feature brooding vampires who impale the heroine and suck her blood are the fastest-growing romance genre.

Surprised? Society is quick to judge the $1 billion men's magazines as immoral, if not downright perverted. But no matter your moral stance, *Maxim* and *Playboy* are to men what romance novels are to women. Both men *and* women have deep primitive-brain desires for sexual stimulation. But women, with their innate preferences for words and emotions, turn to stimulating words to rouse desire. Men, who are hardwired for visual stimulation, prefer pictures.

I am not advocating the use of vampires or steamy stories in your advertising to stir female consumers, or pictures of scantily clad women to make men buy your product, although I think it's clear why these strategies work. The point is that women write and read most romance fiction and erotica. But a magazine featuring nude men has never been much of a hit with women. If you want to capture women's attention and stir their emotions, use their preferred emotional stimulus—words and stories. With men, display a vivid picture.

INTERRUPTIONS, QUESTIONS, NODS, AND BANTER CREATE GENDER BENDERS

Just as misjudging another driver's next move can end in a fender bender, misinterpreting the opposite sex's communication style leads to gender benders. When communicating with the opposite sex, the golden rule does *not* apply. Instead, treat them as *they* prefer to be treated.

Sales Interrupted

Men view communication as a way to solve a problem, and interrupt only to introduce new information, change topics, or disagree—all forms of aggression. Women talk to form bonds and gain consensus; they interrupt to support, agree, or clarify—all forms of empathy.

Women salespeople can improve face-to-face results by merely resisting the urge to interrupt to show support when listening to a man. The interruption—though meant as an act of support—will backfire, as he will interpret your interruption as rude at best, and aggressive at worst. Remember, he does not have four separate areas to "pause" one thought, go to another, and come back to the original thought.

When a Simple Question Can Kill the Sale

A woman will ask questions for advice, to make a connection, and to strengthen another person's commitment to an idea. Many times she already has a firm opinion but is gaining input to build consensus. Contrast that with a man who asks questions for one primary reason—to get an answer. Expect more questions from a woman in the sales and marketing process. She likes to seek out the help of trusted experts. Men, understand that just because she wants your opinion, it's not an indication she is without one of her own.

The Nod

Observe a group of women talking. They look like the most agreeable group of humans ever, each nodding her head in agreement as the others expound. Or so you think. When a woman nods, it does *not* mean that she agrees. It means that she acknowledges your point and that you should continue expressing your thoughts. She is giving you permission to keep talking.

What happens when the nodding stops? You have gone thirty seconds over your allotted time, and you are now rude. Here's the way you can recover. For men this may be the most important advice in the entire book—advice that makes you more successful in sales and marketing . . . and relationships. As soon as you realize the nodding has stopped in your female prospect, say, "Enough about my thoughts; I want to hear how *you* feel about this." Then hush up and listen to what she reveals.

Incessant nodding is not a female conspiracy to give men mixed messages. Complex communication is what sets humans apart from all other species. And it has always been a woman's job to teach children to speak. But listen to a child learning to express herself—one thought can take minutes to complete. A mother constantly encourages her child to talk, patiently nodding whether or not the child makes any sense at all. Women are hardwired to encourage others to continue to communicate by nodding.

To my female readers, take note. If you are a nodder, and most women are, don't nod with your male prospects and clients unless you are agreeing. You do not want to be misconstrued as supportive and then verbally disagree. This is the essence of a mixed message. A woman non-verbally nods and then verbally disapproves, and the man either thinks she has trouble making decisions, or worse, that she is setting him up and cannot be trusted.

And men, you must remember that just because a woman is nodding doesn't mean that she is ready to ink the deal. Old-school sales training has taught us to move in fast when customers indicate they are ready to close the deal. Men, instead of moving in for the close when you get the nod, ask, "Can you see how implementing our solution will provide your department with the efficiencies that you need to meet your strategic objectives?" The question (or another one like it) requires verbal clarification of her thoughts. Half the time, what she tells you won't line up with the equation "nod = yes."

Double Entendres and Getting Beyond the Maybes

The way a woman communicates can confuse a man. She nods even when she might not agree, she asks a question when she knows the answer, and she interrupts with her own story to bond. But when she says, "I'll think about it," guess what? She is really going to think about it.

Contrast this to your male prospect, who is more likely to offer "maybe" as his version of a polite no.

In a selling scenario with a woman who has said she'll think about it, ask if there is any other information you can provide, and when you can follow up with her. Then, provide information that will help her decision-making process, and while she is taking the time to decide, send her a nice note or a reference of someone that reminded you of her. Use the "maybe" season to strengthen your relationship with her.

When a male customer says he wants to think about your service, you need to qualify his statement as an objection. Your job then is to find the true objection and overcome it to keep the prospect engaged. You may even want to simply tell him it's okay to be forthright with you (remember, a comfortable level of communication is foundational to your success). Clearing the air of diplomacy will not only allow him to relax; it will allow you to get straight to the bottom of his hang-up where you can accurately address it.

The One-Up Versus the All-Up

A woman's role as head teacher and comforter of children fosters another communication difference you must beware of when marketing and selling to X or Y. Men bond by bantering, teasing, and using derogatory nicknames. Women don't and never will.

Phil and I invited a few friends over to watch the Fiesta Bowl. As Claude came in the door, he gave a friendly punch to Phil's gut and said, "Hey, looks like you have been enjoying those Heinekens over the holidays."

"Yeah, old man, let's go out and shoot some hoops," Phil replied. "I can still outplay you."

Can you imagine my reaction if Dorie, Claude's wife, had glanced at my waistline and greeted me with, "Wow, you've really been enjoying those Christmas cookies this year!" She'd probably have been watching the Fiesta Bowl alone.

Ads that show men one-upping each other sell beer, deodorant, and shaving cream. Using these tactics with women is the kiss of death in both advertising and face-to-face selling.

Why? Remember from earlier that a woman's life is much easier when there are no scraped elbows *or* bruised egos.

This seems to be the unwritten rule for Y: men who know each other well and respect each other immensely banter in order to bond. I know two very successful CEOs who refer to each other as Lugnut and Chiselchest.

But no matter how well a salesman knows and respects a female client or prospect, calling her a cutesy name (e.g., "Blondie") will usually backfire. Similarly, this is part of the guy's club that the gals should *not* try to join. A woman who attempts to bond by one-upping a man or giving him an endearing derogatory name will break unspoken rules and lose his respect instead of gaining trust.

Bashing the Competition Won't Work for Her

While a woman will tolerate, yet not understand, two men bonding by bantering, she will not put up with a salesperson who bad-mouths the competition. By bashing a competitor—either yours or hers—you will lose more credibility than the rival you're bad-mouthing. However, a fair comparison is welcome. In fact, you can gain her trust by acknowledging a competitor's strong points while making the case for your services as the overall better solution.

As we learned in chapter 2, she is going to do her homework and compare her options. Communicating a fair comparison speaks her verbal language and shows you value her time and intelligence. The simple dialogue will go a long way to earn status as her trusted advisor.

MEN FACE THE WORLD
SHOULDER TO SHOULDER

With twenty-seven seconds left in the half, it's fourth down and inches to the goal, and your team, down by four points, is going for it. Then the snap is fumbled, and the other team recovers and runs ninety-eight yards for a touchdown. With their heads hanging, your team returns to the sidelines. What is the coach doing? He is yelling in their faces. This is a time for confrontation, not camaraderie.

But when your team returns to the field after halftime, it's a different scene. The quarterback and coach stand shoulder to shoulder, reviewing the playbook and looking out at the field together. The team's quest is to win on the field—there they foster open and unhindered lines of communication so each play and player is precise and in concert. When they are discussing the strategy for success, coaches and players often stand next to each other, facing the field, or in a circle, staring at a whiteboard or the ground. In every case, they are shoulder to shoulder and not eye to eye. In contrast, when someone messes up—or drops the ball— and there is less immediate concern for feelings or goodwill, the conversation gets aggressive, and men face each other.

Where your sales and marketing communication is concerned, the point is this: men are less comfortable with eye contact than women and would prefer you to not sit or stand directly in front of them. In contrast, being comfortable with eye contact is wired into female brains. As stated previously, twenty-four hours after birth, an infant girl prefers to gaze at a human face, while a baby boy prefers to watch a mobile. Testosterone seems to be the deciding factor of the distinction. Cambridge University psychologist Dr.

Simon Baron-Cohen filmed one-year-old children at play and measured the amount of eye contact they made with their mothers, all of whom had undergone amniocentesis during pregnancy. The more testosterone (measured during the amniocentesis) the children had been exposed to in the womb, the less likely they were to make eye contact at one year of age. Men have higher levels of testosterone than women, and men with the highest testosterone levels are more likely to view eye contact as confrontational.

Position yourself next to, not across from, a male customer; then look out at the product (car, computer, house) or plan, and paint a vivid picture of success. This is the most comfortable posture of communication and will help earn his trust.

WOMEN TACKLE THE
WORLD FACE-TO-FACE

Women have been peering into their babies' eyes at close range ever since there were mothers and babies. In contrast to men, women are not only comfortable with eye contact; they demand it.

Susan and her husband, John, approached me after a recent presentation. As empty nesters, they had just completed their dream home. Susan described the meetings with their builder. "John and the contractor would stand next to each other," she bemoaned, "eyes gazing at the construction site while discussing the plans. When I wanted to add something to the conversation, I would step in front of the builder, look up, and speak. He would then maneuver his body so I was no longer in front of him, break my gaze, and reply. Every time we met with him, I felt like I was dancing in front of him to get his attention. My frustration built, and halfway through the project, I began to dislike him and dread the next meeting. Now I realize he is one of those high-testosterone men who is uncomfortable with prolonged eye contact." I nodded.

Sit across from your female customer and look into her eyes—not over her shoulder—while discussing your service. The most important part of the interaction will be the relationship that you build.

BRAIN ACTIVITY DURING SPEECH
(Drawings depict brain activity shown by the shading from fMRI studies.)

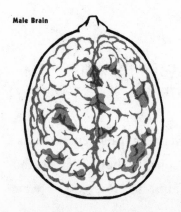

Male Brain

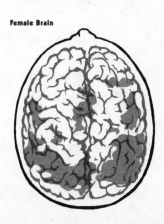

Female Brain

	Male	Female
Areas Stimulated During Speech	Two diffuse areas on the left hemisphere.	Two specific areas on the left hemisphere.
		Two specific areas on the right hemisphere.
		Eleven percent more neurons in areas associated with language.
Traits	Larger vocabulary; likes use of jargon.	More proficient at talking, listening, writing, use of vocabulary.
	Interrupts to introduce information, change topics, or disagree.	Interrupts to encourage or clarify.
	Nods to show agreement.	Nods to show acknowledgment.
	More likely to prepare a public speech.	Speaks freely in a safe network of colleagues or friends.
	Cannot listen while speaking.	Can speak and listen at the same time.
	Communicates to give directives or banter.	Communicates to gain consensus.
	Avoids asking questions, as it shows weakness and an appeal for help.	Asks questions not for advice so much as to make a connection.
An "Aha" Moment	Cannot process multiple conversations; dismisses simultaneous conversations as mindless chatter.	Can have multiple, simultaneous conversations.

TAKING COMMUNICATION SMARTS
TO THE STREETS

The differences in X and Y verbal wiring generate mis-understandings that unintentionally sabotage sales—and subsequently customer relationships. Your job is to be attuned to these differences and modify your style to maximize your message and minimize misunderstandings. Do so in the following ways:

X: When selling to her, let the conversation bloom and grow many petals. She is at home with multiple topics on the table and will, over time, tie them together. If you're discussing the color of stain for her hardwood floor, don't try to refocus the conversation if she brings up her dogs and the need to have their nails trimmed. She's just talking through the many ways the buy might affect her life. Listen to these cues and treat them as opportunities to earn her trust through active listening, and position your product as the right solution for her nest. Don't read her nodding as a signal to close the deal—she does this only to tell you she's listening. If she says she'll think about it, she really wants to think about it. Offer her resources for getting her questions answered, and ask her when she'd like you to follow up. While she's thinking everything through, send her a nice note to further earn her trust and make the process of communicating with you comfortable.

Y: When selling to him, avoid unfocused conversations where the primary topic changes every thirty seconds. He prefers to only communicate when necessary and in order to meet a precise goal. If the discussion is about a riding mower, don't talk about the weather and how the local baseball team did last night. Multiple topics in a single conversation are mindless chatter to him and can leave him frustrated, impatient, and eventually uninterested. Listen to his objections, because he will offer them—in some cases interrupting you to do so—but if he says maybe, he likely means no. Get to the bottom of his maybe by allowing him the freedom to express the objection on his mind, but don't interrupt him—he might translate it as overly aggressive. You'll know if you've succeeded in winning his business—his nodding is confirmation of his agreement.

THE ECONOMICS OF EMOTION

He contains his feelings; she conveys hers.

A group of eighteen surgeons identify a perfect spot to consolidate their three offices into one and develop their own surgery center. This patient-friendly option (better parking, access, and convenience of services) would significantly lower overhead while boosting revenue from new service lines, providing each surgeon with the opportunity to increase his or her personal income by 15 to 20 percent.

Because only some of the partners have the ability to invest in the real estate, they wrangle over lease terms. The impasse causes the deal to die. Everybody loses. What went wrong?

Finance 101 teaches us that in order to make good financial decisions, people should:

- make logical, rational, self-interested decisions that weigh costs against benefits and maximize value and profit;
- be intelligent and analytic creatures possessing perfect self-regulation in pursuit of future goals; and
- ignore feelings and emotions in decisions.

These views certainly help build academic theories, but there is one big flaw in this teaching—real people do not act in these ways.

In the true example above, eleven of the eighteen surgeons could not afford to participate in the purchase of the property. While the remaining seven had the resources to fund the project, after a vote the partners decided that they did not want to create a situation in which some partners were leasing space from a few of the other partners.

Bottom line: while everyone would benefit from this new business model, those who could not also make money on the real estate stopped the deal because they didn't want their more financially sound partners to have a better financial arrangement.

Joy, contempt, fear, lust, greed, and in the example above, an underlying envy that someone is getting a much better deal ("it's not fair") impacts retail purchases as well as business transactions on a daily basis. Emotions reside in the heads of your male and female customers. These feelings affect the decisions they make regarding you, how they feel about your offering, and whether they pass on your product or become a lifelong customer. And by now you know one strategy does not fit all—men and women "feel" differently and must therefore be sold to differently.

Women have long been stereotyped as the more emotional gender. Now brain scientists have determined that the emotional wiring of the sexes is indeed different. Men and women use different brain networks to process and remember emotional events. Because these networks are also influenced by varying levels of sex hormones, your customer's emotional response to you and your offering will be fundamentally unique depending on the customer's sex.

Wouldn't it be wonderful if you could realize the dream of morphing every qualified prospect into a customer who then turns into a repeat client and with time becomes a lifelong advocate and partner? To accomplish this, you must create and build trust while connecting to your customers' emotions. It sounds so simple, but if it were, more would be doing it. Read on to learn the unique nuances you must heed along the path to building strong relationships with either gender.

NOTHING MORE THAN FEELINGS

News flash: men are better than women at containing their emotions. In men, emotion is confined to two specific areas on the right hemisphere of the brain. Language is located on the left hemisphere, and men have fewer neurons connecting the two hemispheres. The result? Men have an innate ability to compartmentalize emotions, while women are endowed with an inherent ability (or some might say a "need") to express them.

Couple this structural difference with the unique chemicals that fuel the male and female brains and you must conclude that a gender-specific sales strategy is imperative for winning the hearts of all your customers.

HE TRUSTS HIS INSTITUTIONS

One of the most difficult challenges salespeople face is to engage a prospect's initial interest—at least enough to obtain an introductory appointment. In most cases you start as a stranger. In many instances your customer is completely unfamiliar with your company and product. So how do you break the ice? How do you gain the trust necessary to have an initial conversation about your offering? The answer: belong to your customer's "in-group."

According to Marilyn Brewer, a psychology professor at Ohio State University, most Americans trust strangers *if* they belong to what they consider their "in-group."[1] But Professor Brewer's study found that men and women define their in-groups differently.

Study participants (students at OSU) were told they would either be given $3 from the researchers or an undisclosed amount (which turned out to be $11) from one of three strangers. If they opted for the undisclosed amount, the students were then asked to choose the stranger from which they would be given the money.

Stranger One: another Ohio State student
Stranger Two: attended another university at
     which the participant had a friend
Stranger Three: attended another university at
     which the participant knew no one

The male participants were much likelier to trust a stranger that was a fellow Ohio State student than a stranger from other schools, even those at which they knew someone. Men tend to trust people that share an objective group membership. The male participants were quoted as saying things like, "Someone from Ohio State would not let me down."

Men value their group or team. "You see this in male-dominated groups, like the military or football teams

—there's a clear distinction between "us" and "them," Brewer says.[2]

Advertisers and salespeople can gain initial credibility with a male prospect by belonging to his group. If you are an alumnus of the same college, or a member of the same church, community group, rotary club, or association, use this membership to fuel your initial introduction. If you are not a member in his club, find someone in your company who is, or consider joining your prospect's group.

SHE TRUSTS HER CONNECTIONS

Where men tend to trust strangers in their clubs, companies, or teams, women trust strangers who share a personal connection—a friend of a friend, or a friend of a family member. The female OSU students in Professor Brewer's study predominantly chose to receive the money from a stranger from another university where they had a friend.

When making your initial prospecting call to a woman, it will mean more if you have a common friend or acquaintance than if you are both members of an organization. "Our mutual friend Nancy recommended that we meet" will go a lot further than "I understand that we are both members of the local Chamber of Commerce" in gaining your female prospect's trust.

MEN ARE WIRED FOR ACTION

Deep inside both hemispheres in both the male and female brains are almond-shaped clusters of neurons called *amygdalas*. The amygdala plays a pivotal role in processing hormone and other involuntary functions, such as your response to fear and aggression. And in a man, the amygdala talks with specific brain regions that help him quickly respond to sensors that tell him what is going on *outside* the body that requires action.[3]

In other words, a man is wired to move. He responds to external problems by taking action. To become a trusted advisor to your male customer, determine the challenges he faces, and then help him formulate an action plan to conquer those challenges. You will be speaking directly to his decision-making emotions.

WOMEN ARE WIRED FOR CONNECTION

If you were able to peer inside a woman's brain, you would find her amygdalas precisely in the same spots and looking just like her brother's. However, this cluster of neurons in her, so important in regulating emotions, communicates with the insular cortex and the hypothalamus—brain regions that respond to sensors *inside* the body and help her regulate hormones, heart rate, blood pressure, digestion, and respiration.[4]

"Women," explains Larry Cahill of the University of California–Irvine, "have [always] had to deal with a number of internal stressors, such as childbirth, that men haven't had to experience. What is fascinating about this is the brain seems to have evolved to be in tune with those different stressors."[5]

While male customers will feel the need to discuss, or better yet implement, a plan of action, your female customer will first feel the need to discuss how she and her team feel about the problem to be solved and how they perceive your offering. Instead of pushing an action plan, engage her primary emotions by initiating a conversation about what she senses to be problematic. Ask how she and her team are coping with the situation, and then offer a solution that promises harmony to her and her network of associates—she will want to calm nerves.

IN STRESS HE'LL FIGHT OR FLY

In Psychology 101, we were taught that animals and humans instinctively resort to fight or flight in situations of danger. And this tenet is true for about half the population—men. Whether he is cornered by a saber-tooth tiger or his current pit-bull-of-a-boss, in stressful situations the male body responds by pumping blood and oxygen to his reptilian brain, where the fight-or-flight action is controlled.

This means that your male customer is more likely to either take immediate action in response to an emergency or leave the building, solve the problem alone in seclusion, and then come back to implement a solution. This is also why when my husband, Phil, has had a tough week at the office and there are a thousand things to do over the weekend just to catch up, he will respond by taking a nap. The efficient male brain allows him to take a short rest and reenergize to tackle the stress yet to come.

Whether you are with your husband, coworker, or customer, resist the urge to encourage a man to talk while under stress. This only increases his stress level. Let him have his space to retreat, work out the problem privately, or rest to reenergize. Then when he is ready to act, position yourself to be a pivotal part of his action team.

IN STRESS, SHE'LL TEND AND BEFRIEND

Nearly seventy years after psychologist Walter Cannon proposed that stress triggers the human response of lashing out or running away, Dr. Shelley Taylor, a psychology professor at UCLA, and her colleagues challenged the fight-or-flight theory. Knowing that past stress studies rarely involved females, Taylor's team wondered if women responded differently than men to stress. They reasoned that the adaptive value of fighting or fleeing might be lower for females, who often have dependent young and subsequently risk more if injured or displaced. Additionally, they knew that females of many species form tight, stable alliances, possibly reflecting an adaptive tendency in stress to seek out friends for support.[6]

After combing through thirty years of studies on stress, Taylor's team found that compared to males, females' physical aggression and fear-related behaviors are less intense and more "cerebral"—they are displayed in response to specific circumstances and are less tied to physiological arousal. So while both sexes share the capacity for fight or flight, females seem to use it less.[7]

Instead, during tough times, stressed females spend significantly more time tending to vulnerable offspring than males. Studies by psychologist Rena Repetti in the late 1990s showed that after a hard day at work, women were much more nurturing toward their children, whereas men withdrew from family life. The researchers suspect that endorphins—proteins that help alleviate pain—and oxytocin—a female reproductive hormone—play an important role in establishing this pattern, while factors like learning and socialization help to maintain it.[8]

Both oxytocin and endorphins may also contribute to

the second piece of the puzzle—females' tendency to "befriend." In many mammals, and cross-culturally in humans, females form especially close, stable attachments with other females, often kin. And this tendency for females to affiliate with other familiar people increases during times of stress. Taylor's team concluded that befriending is "the primary gender difference in adult human behavioral responses to stress."[9]

So when your female client is overwhelmed, she'll relieve her tension by tending—which can be anything from cleaning up the break room to finalizing the most recent business plan. This attention to getting things in order and taking care of loose ends brings a sense of control and accomplishment to a frazzled female. Once she starts to bring order to a task, she'll also want to befriend, which is the code word for "talk." She will want to talk through her problem and the various scenarios on the telephone, over lunch, or while tending.

Be there to listen when a female customer is stressed or overwhelmed, without immediately trying to solve the problem. She first feels the need to talk through all of the options. And by all means offer to help with the tasks of tending if it is within your means to do so. The female multitasker will feel more efficient if she is able to tidy up the mess while talking through her alternatives. If you can truly help her during this emotional process, you will go a long way toward solidifying her trust. And ultimately her trust will close the deal.

FORBIDDEN TEARS

When women think sad thoughts, they show eight times more brain activity than men.[10] This high activity level, located throughout both hemispheres, explains why women can and do express emotions while performing almst any activity. Unfortunately, this expression may often take the form of crying—the most misunderstood reaction in the world.

Crying is the ultimate forbidden act in business. Women know it, do everything in the world to avoid it, and—daggonit—there's still not a professional woman I have spoken to that has not broken down at least one time in her career and cried in front of a male colleague, or worse, a client. Women cry when sad, mad, happy, and sometimes, during a commercial. While crying, they may feel silly and guilty, but it's a reaction that seems unstoppable.

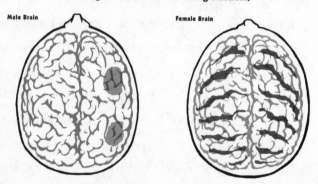

BRAIN ACTIVITY DURING EMOTIONS
(Drawings depict brain activity shown by the shading from fMRI studies during emotion.)

Male Brain   Female Brain

	Male	Female
During peak "emotional" moments	Two specific areas on the right hemisphere light up.	Widespread activity shown across both hemispheres. When thinking sad thoughts, her brain is eight times more active.
Traits	Exhibits less eye contact.	Exhibits intense eye contact.
	Shorter attention span.	Longer attention span.
	Higher sensation seeking.	Lower sensation seeking.
	Needs more space.	Needs less space.
	Maintains more distance from others of the same sex.	Maintains less distance from others of the same sex.
	Quicker to anger; exhibited in fight-or-flight response.	Slower to anger; may exhibit by crying.
Conclusion	Men have highly contained emotional centers on the right hemisphere and highly contained verbal centers on the left, with much less connection between hemispheres than women. Men need more time to realize and verbalize their emotions.	In women, widespread emotional activity is shown throughout the brain, coupled with strong verbal centers on both sides of the brain. Women are highly attuned to their emotions and will typically verbalize their feelings.

DRY EYES

Men, on the other hand, rarely cry. Short of hearing of the death of a close loved one, or losing a limb, it's hard to imagine a man crying at work. When a man shows emotion, it is more likely to be anger and expressed by a fight-or-flight response. When a woman cries, a man dismisses her as overreactive and weak at best, hysterical and manipulating at worst.

But the truth is that women can't help it. The hormone prolactin is partially responsible for that oft-cited and much-maligned difference between men and women: tears. Prolactin directs the body to grow breasts and tear ducts, and to produce breast milk. A woman has 60 percent more prolactin than a man. Couple prolactin with a brain that is hardwired to feel a full range of emotions, and the spontaneous response is tears.

While crying is a natural way women deal with stress, it—like lashing out in anger—can sabotage a career. My female readers may find these steps helpful in overcoming the waterfall effect:

- *Fight:* Try not to succumb to tears in the workplace. If you feel them coming on, take a deep breath in, and look up to the left so the left hemisphere of your brain kicks in—hopefully stemming the flow of tears. Let your breath out slowly and entirely. Releasing your breath actually lowers your blood pressure.
- *Activate* the right side of your body. You may look strange looking up and to your left, so instead engage the left side of your brain by wiggling your toes on your right foot. And—I know this sounds silly, but you know how humiliating it is to cry at work—*concentrate* on wiggling your toes.
- *Educate* men and women about the different ways

that the sexes respond to stress. If you are in HR, make this a corporate education goal.

- *Flight:* Resist the urge to talk through the problem with a man. If you can't stop the tears from falling, excuse yourself with, "I'd like to think about this and get back with you tomorrow." Release the stress privately or find a woman's shoulder for support.

- *Fight tears with water:* If you know that you will be in a stressful situation, be armed with a glass of water. Take many sips and swallow frequently. The act of swallowing makes it hard to cry.

WITH HIM,
HELP IS A LAST RESORT

How many times have you met someone at a business function, asked what the person did, and five minutes later he or she was still talking? To make matters worse, you still couldn't tell another person in the room what the loquacious one did for a living, and you wondered if the poor soul knew. If you find yourself on the other side of this situation, being asked what you do for a living, keep your answer clear and concise. In short, develop your thirty-second story. Twenty seconds would be better, and fifteen seconds, outstanding. Here's why: most sales pitches and ad campaigns initially have only that brief clip of time to captivate an audience.

What would you say if a top prospect plopped down in front of you and said, "You have thirty seconds to answer . . . What can you do for me?" I'm sure you've considered the question before, but have you thought about whether your brief answer triggers the right emotions in your male and/or female prospects?

When asked to give their thirty-second elevator speech, many salespeople begin the pitch with, "I help companies . . ." If your pitch begins with those three words, change them now. You are alienating both X and Y right out of the gate.

First, half of your audience—the men—don't want help. Your male client values independence and action. To a man, needing help is a sign of weakness, and providing help—as opposed to action—is anemic. Help is a weasel word. So when you say, "I help companies . . . ," you are both insulting him by implying that he needs help and sabotaging your credibility by minimizing your impact. Instead, craft your male-geared elevator speech (as well as all your other business language in ads, on Web sites, in e-mails, etc.) with action and results in mind. Try these hard-driving statements instead:

I implement . . .
I build . . .

I challenge . . .

I discover . . .

I create . . .

I explore . . .

I perform . . .

I execute . . .

I accomplish . . .

I complete . . .

I achieve . . .

I fix . . .

TO HER, TO HELP IS TO CARE

While help is a four-letter word to men, women are not offended by an offer of assistance. She doesn't respond to your pitch, "I help companies . . . ," because she doesn't care about companies or institutions; she cares about *people*. If you want to win the right to continue discussing business with a female prospect, tell her, "I help people . . ."

Thomas J. Moyer, Ohio's chief justice, describes America's story: "The American story is the story of people who reach beyond themselves."[11] Doesn't that sum it all up? Did that create a vision of people who risked everything to cross oceans, climb mountains, and fly to the moon—people who are still reaching out and providing hope to the many corners of the world?

Chief Justice Moyer's American story is about people, not a country. When speaking to your female prospects, also make your story about people, not a company, technology, or product.

Now, you may be wondering, *Do I need two gender-specific pitches?* No, of course not. You need one strong thirty-second—better yet, fifteen-second—story that portrays action and results (a man's first priority), and a benefit to people (the priority always on the top of a woman's mind). First, strike all weasel words—*help*, *assist*, and *facilitate*—and replace them with action, results-oriented words, like the examples presented earlier. Then talk about the effects you have on people or the team. Once you have something you like, eliminate any unnecessary words. Challenge yourself to get your elevator speech to fewer than twenty seconds. Your story should incite an emotional response from your prospect. You want him and her to respond with, "Tell me more."

TAKING EMOTION SMARTS TO THE STREET

When it comes down to it, we're all emotional creatures. The difference lies in how those emotions are triggered and then how they affect us as men and women. Knowing the keys to triggering the right emotions and avoiding the wrong ones is critical to all effective marketing and selling. Here's what you need to remember to do with each gender.

X: Since she trusts her connections with people, finding a link to the friends, colleagues, or family members of your female prospect will earn you an early measure of trust. When you begin talking business, don't push a plan of action with her as you would your male prospects. She will first feel the need to discuss how she and/or her team feel about the problem. Engage her primary emotions by initiating a conversation about what she senses to be problematic. If you sense she's stressed, be there to listen, and put problem-solving on hold. Her tending tendency will make her feel the need to talk through all of the options and tidy things up in her mind. She may also want to physically tidy her surroundings or even make a phone call to tidy up her nest. Encourage her to do such things, as it eases her mind. And if you can offer her help with her tending, you will go a long way toward solidifying her trust. And ultimately her trust that you're all about helping people—specifically, her and her nest-mates—will close the deal.

Y: Since he places high value in institution membership, find a way to tie into one of your male prospect's groups. If he's a member of the skeet-shooting club just outside of town, buy yourself a rifle and some orange disks and go join. He's quicker to feel he can trust you if you share a group affiliation. When his challenge comes up in discussion, lead the conversation to talking about the proper action plan to solve it. Don't make the mistake of telling him you'll help. Needing help makes him feel weak or inadequate, and to offer it to him is to tell him you think it's true. If you find he is stressed in the buying process, give him space. You won't get anywhere with a stressed male prospect if you push forward with your agenda. He'll either turn defensive or walk out. Respect his space. Then when he's ready to return to the business at hand, he'll feel that you and your product can be trusted.

PART 2

GenderCycle Selling™

If you weren't already, I hope by now you are convinced that your male and female customers have unique neural networks and, therefore, unique decision-making processes. In order to connect with both sexes each time you market and sell, you must obviously approach and communicate with X and Y differently throughout the sales cycle. While the many factors we've already discussed will come into play, in chapter 9 we'll map out the details of the step-by-step process of getting X to buy. Then in chapter 10, we'll walk through the same process for Y. In the end, you'll possess the tools to be an effective seller or marketer with both sexes.

THE X OF BUY

Q: Why can't a woman be more like a man?

A: Henry Higgins, the arrogant professor of phonetics in *My Fair Lady*, probably wasn't the first to ask this question. Thankfully, we don't have to any longer. An international team of scientists led by the Wellcome Trust Sanger Institute near Cambridge, England, found the irrefutable answer. In 2005, these researchers first mapped the X chromosome—one of the two coils of DNA that determine gender. Their studies revealed that Homo sapiens (you and me) boast not one genome—the full DNA sequence of an organism—but two: both male and female.[1] So while men and women are without a doubt from the same planet, the answer to Henry Higgins's (and, perhaps, your) question is simple: a woman can't be like a man, and vice versa, because we are as different as members of the same species can be.

The X chromosome has close to one thousand working genes. Doubly blessed with the X, scientists previously thought that each woman's extra X chromosome entirely switched off in every cell, thereby preventing duplicate genetic instructions. They also assumed that the paltry eighty-six genes on the male Y chromosome were the only genetic barrier between men and women. But this study showed that up to 25 percent of a woman's second X gene remains active, giving her a "double dose of X" that could have important effects.

"Our study shows that the inactive X in women is not as silent as we thought," said Laura Carrel of Pennsylvania State University, who led this element of the research. "The effects of these genes from the inactive X chromosome could explain some of the differences between men and women that are not attributable to sex hormones."[2]

Carrel's coresearcher, Hunt Willard of Duke University, further explained: "We now know that 25 percent of the X chromosome—200 to 300 genes—can be uniquely expressed in one sex relative to the other. In essence, there is not one human genome, but two—male and female."[3]

Here is the real kicker—the researchers found that

many of these genes also vary in their pattern of expression from woman to woman. This means that women are less genetically similar to one another than are men, and that may contribute to individuals' behavior or susceptibility to disease.[4]

So what does this mean to you, whose livelihood is determined by selling? You need to better understand how these differences play out during the sales cycle—your customers' decision processes—so that you can best connect to your female prospects and customers. Read on to understand GenderCycle Selling™ and how to apply what you have learned in the first eight chapters when selling face-to-face to a woman.

GENDERCYCLE SELLING™: THE X SALES CYCLE

The traditional sales cycle has six key phases that are focused on what you, the salesperson, should do during each step in the cycle. Virtually every sales interaction will follow these phases, whether it lasts several minutes or several months. GenderCycle Selling™ focuses not only on what you, the salesperson, do during each phase but on *what your customer is thinking* at each of these key phases. By understanding her values, preferences, and thought processes, you can adapt your sales approach to attract her attention to your product or service, shorten the sales cycle, close more sales, and build long-term relationships with your female clients. In the GenderCycle Selling™ X sales cycle:

You're . . .	And *she's . . .*
1. Prospecting	1. Searching
2. Questioning and listening	2. Talking and trying to bond
3. Presenting	3. Synthesizing and empathizing
4. Overcoming objections	4. Seeking assurance
5. Closing the sale	5. Solidifying the relationship
6. Promoted to trusted advisor	6. The integrator and influencer

SALES SCENARIOS

Now let's run through the X sales cycle using two hypotheti-
cal sales scenarios. The first is a business-to-business (B2B)
situation, and the second is a retail or direct-to-consumer
(D2C) example. While there is no possible way to address
every different type of sales scenario, a B2B sales cycle typically goes through *all* of these steps. If you are in retail or
D2C sales, you may not go through every one of these steps;
however, the same techniques will work.

B2B

- You are Joe, a salesperson (either male or female)
  for ABC Solutions, a company providing technology
  networking solutions.
- Your prospect is Samantha, the chief technology
  officer for XYZ Inc., a local provider of personal
  and corporate insurance services.
- Your goal is to create the shortest path to identifying
  a qualified prospect and then creating a loyal lifetime
  client using the tools you've learned in *The X and Y
  of Buy*.

Retail or D2C

- You are Joe, a financial planner (either male or
  female) for ABC Solutions.

- Your prospect is Samantha, the chief technology officer for XYZ Inc., a local provider of personal and corporate insurance services, married and mother of two children, ages eight and ten.
- Your goal is to create the shortest path to identifying a qualified prospect and then creating a loyal lifetime client using the tools you've learned in *The X and Y of Buy*.

So here we go, Joe. Armed with your knowledge of what makes Samantha tick, let's go through the X sales cycle.

PHASE ONE: YOU'RE PROSPECTING; SHE'S SEARCHING

Finding qualified prospects for your products or services is the natural first step in the sales process. Whether you sell products in retail or sell high-tech business solutions, you must identify your target market, understand their needs, and position your product or services as the best solution.

The following steps will help you connect to women during your first phase of selling: prospecting. At this point, your female prospect, Samantha, is searching—while she may not know you, your company, or your service, and might not even realize that she has a need for your product, she is always searching. Her brain is like a rotating light-house, never resting, looking for people and things that relate and will enhance her nest. Position your product as her answer to making life easier or providing greater harmony in her relationships.

1. Capture Samantha's attention

- Relate to her everyday life.
- Promote harmony and an easier life.
- Help the people she touches.
- Feature other customers like her.
- Support her as an influencer.

2. Empathize with her nest

Once you've identified Samantha as the decision maker or influencer when it comes to making purchases for her company or family, you must learn all you can about her unique mission before you approach her. Then at each contact you will uncover more about what makes her tick. When you understand her nest—the group or place in which she wants to wield positive influence—you can then plan your sales approach to position your product or service as an integral relationship builder.

How do you find out about Samantha? Search the Internet, looking for articles, clubs, and organizations that she supports. Then use your network of friends and business associates. A five-minute conversation with someone who has worked with Samantha or is her neighbor or is a mutual friend will provide invaluable insight.

3. Make first contact

Once you have identified Samantha as your gal, contact her. One of the most common initial contacts is a "cold call" conducted by phone or in person. My definition of a cold call is any contact with a prospect in which she has not indicated that she wants you to call. These tips will help you turn your *cold calls* into *warm female prospects*:

- *Find her friends*—the women and men in whom she trusts and confides. In chapter 8, you learned that women trust people who know a friend of theirs—better yet, women trust a *friend of a friend* of theirs. Her nest consists of her family members, friends, and close colleagues at work. Your best introduction to a woman will come not from you but from one of her female friends who provides an introduction. It's not that she trusts her female friends more than her male friends—the introduction will mean the same from either sex. It is just much easier to get a woman to make an introduction. As natural networkers and facilitators of relationships, women like introducing their friends and colleagues, so her friend will often be happy to oblige. Ask her to introduce the two of you. If her friend is too busy to make the introduction on your time frame, ask her if you can e-mail Samantha, using the friend's name as the connector, and carbon copy the friend on the correspondence.

- *Relate with an experience.* If you can't find a mutual friend or acquaintance to provide an introduction, draw on similar experiences to relate to your female prospect. For example, you may both travel abroad frequently or enjoy working out at the local gym. Discuss your shared experience and the feelings that experience evoked to bond with your female prospect. If you have a friend's introduction *and* a common experience, use both to connect.

- *Know your call objective.* Your purpose may be to obtain an appointment, to qualify the lead, to question, or to ask for an introduction to a certain person. No matter what, you should be gaining permission to get to the next step.

- *Send a concise letter or e-mail introduction* with your Web site link and a compelling reason for speaking with you— how you or your product relate to her. Detail the date that you will be calling her and what you hope will happen after the call. Here's an example of a concise e-mail to Samantha, CTO for XYZ Inc., from you, Joe, with ABC Solutions. This example e-mail is entirely female focused on personal relationships and experiences, and therefore resonates with women:

Dear Samantha,

Our mutual friend Susan Smith gave me your name and e-mail address. She said that the two of you vacationed together with your families at Disney World last year after the RIMS conference. I was asking her for pointers for my upcoming Disney trip with my children, and she encouraged me to contact you, as we have many things in common.

Susan has been my client and friend for the last three years. I have worked with Susan and her team to achieve their phenomenal growth in IT networking. I'd love to get together for lunch or coffee in the near future. If it's okay, I will call you next Thursday to arrange a time. In the meantime, please do not hesitate to contact me if you should have any questions.

Joe Smith
Director of Sales (B2B)/Financial Planner (D2C)
ABC Solutions
Domain
E-mail
Phone
Making Your Business Hum with IT Solutions (B2B)/
Making Your Dreams a Reality Through Financial
    Planning (D2C)

Make it easy for your female or male prospects to know who you are by providing a quick link to your company's Web site. Everyone—and especially every salesperson—should have an automatic e-mail signature that includes his or her name, title, company, Web site link, e-mail address, and phone number. Make your message easy on the eyes: use black font, size 11 or 12.

- *Make the call.* On Thursday, with your notes and your calendar in front of you, make the call. "Samantha, this is Joe, Susan Smith's friend. Tuesday I sent an e-mail to you to see if we could work in a time for coffee or lunch in the next couple of weeks. I am going to be in your area next Wednesday the 24th, and the following Monday the 29th. Are you available either of those days?"

The above introductory e-mail and opening phone call immediately state your relationship with Samantha through your mutual friend Susan, denote a shared personal experience, and ask for a time to share coffee or food—code words for "Let's talk."

Notice I did not open with "Did you get the e-mail that I sent?" This allows the prospect to simply say no, just to avoid further contact. Well-thought-out phrasing can allow you to further your sales opportunity instead of hitting a dead end.

PHASE TWO: THE FIRST MEETING—
YOU'RE QUESTIONING AND LISTENING;
SHE'S TALKING AND TRYING TO BOND

For many salespeople, this is the hardest part of the sales cycle. By definition, a great salesperson is enthusiastic about his or her product and anxious to provide his or her company's product or solution. And during the second phase of selling to X—the first meeting (or if you are selling cars or a product that may be sold in one encounter, the first part of the encounter)—there is one cardinal rule: *remember that you are gathering information from the prospect, not selling.* To put it simply: you are listening, not talking.

By following the steps that follow, you will gain both Samantha's first level of trust and the information you need to position you and your product as a critical component of Samantha's network.

During this phase, Samantha is talking and discovering if you have the ability to understand and, more important, empathize with her situation. Subconsciously she is deciding if you are a good listener and have the ability to understand both her needs and the individual needs of her nest. Here's how to bond.

Assume the position

During the meeting, you must be friendly and professional while relating on a personal level. A woman's professional life is highly integrated with her personal life. You might be the best sales and service person delivering the best solution in your industry, but you had better conduct your personal life with integrity, because she does not compartmentalize the two. Position yourself across from Samantha, maintaining eye contact. Do not look across her shoulder. Women have an amazing ability to read nuances. She will notice your diverted gaze and think that you are not devoting your full attention to her.

Ask questions that resonate with women

Encourage Samantha's innate desire to bond by asking open-ended questions that encourage her to reveal her current situation and her feelings about its implications and solutions. Emphasize her team. Great questions for Samantha:

B2B: "The article in the paper about XYZ's growth was fascinating. What key people or factors contributed to the growth? How has the growth affected the people in your department and your customers?"

"You are clearly positioned to launch your company to the next level. What resources will your team need to accomplish your goals?"

"Tell me about the hurdles or obstacles in your team's way."

"Looking out on the horizon, what would success look like for you and the people you work with in one year, three years, and five years?"

"How would you personally like to influence your company and the people that depend on you?"

D2C: "I work with many women who are high-powered executives, community leaders, and mothers. Many wish that they had more time to devote to planning their financial future, including funding their kids' college expenses and their own retirements. What are you currently doing to plan for your future needs, and are you comfortable that this plan will provide for those needs?"

"What will your family need to do differently to make sure that you have the money to provide college expenses and a wonderful retirement for you and your husband?"

"Tell me about the hurdles or obstacles in your family's way."

"Looking out on the horizon, what would success look like for your family in one year, five years, ten years, and ten-year increments after?"

"How would you like to influence and provide for your philanthropic interests in the future?"

If you are a man, nod occasionally to show you understand. If you are a woman, the nodding comes naturally.

Tell a story that shows that you have experienced her situation. *Do not provide the solution* at this point. If you do, you risk alienating her. She just wants you to understand and verify her feelings about her current situation, not provide the solution.

This is the time to interject, "I know exactly how you feel. That happened to me . . ." A related story shows empathy. However, if you do not have a similar story, don't make one up. A woman can spot an insincere story or compliment a mile away and will quickly dismiss you as a cad. Listening attentively is far more appealing than a confabulated story made up for effect.

During the meeting be sincere and friendly. Humor always helps a personal interaction. Just a chuckle helps release serotonin in the brain, which stimulates feelings of goodwill. But do not make fun of anyone else, including your competition or hers. For X, humor is not humor if it comes at the expense of someone else.

Close with action

Take note; you are now closing the meeting, and you still haven't talked about your product, solution, or company. Congratulations, you did it! You listened to Samantha and conveyed that you thoroughly understand and empathize with her situation. Now is the time to make a final statement that builds rapport and confidence that you can be trusted.

B2B: "Samantha, I appreciate your time and enjoyed hearing the story of you and your associates at XYZ. My colleagues at ABC and I are uniquely positioned to work with you to launch your services regionally. We can be your network partners to ensure that you obtain your goal to become the industry leader in three years. We both realize it will be hard work, but with the right plan—and ABC supporting your team—we'll achieve your goals and help your team be more productive in the future. I am going to share the goals and obstacles that we discussed today with the people on my team and develop a plan. Can we pick a date next week when I can bring my team in and present our plan to you and your colleagues?"

D2C: "Samantha, I appreciate your time and enjoyed getting to know you. I appreciate your family's current situation and the goals you have for the future. Having my own family and career, I understand how you can wake up ten years later and realize that you are behind in your financial plan to fund college expenses and retirement. I would like to put together a plan to ensure that you obtain all of your financial goals. The first step is for us to gather more detailed information about your present situation and all of the things that may impact your financial future. This step will be the most time-consuming for you but very necessary. May I send a questionnaire to you today for you to complete? Once completed, I will need about a week to review it with your goals in mind and come back with suggestions. If that sounds good, let's go ahead and schedule an appointment in three weeks to go over my suggestions."

Once you confirm the date and time, it's time to plan your presentation.

PHASE THREE: YOU'RE PRESENTING; SHE'S SYNTHESIZING AND EMPATHIZING

Presenting your solution is the favorite phase of the sales cycle for most salespeople. Now is the time you get to talk about how you can help. But most important, now is the time Samantha will learn whether you really listened in Phase Two—if you have done your homework and can empathize and build relationships with all the members of her team or family.

Phase Three is the first time you will be doing the majority of talking. While your female prospect is listening, she will also be synthesizing—combining your service and ideas with different situations into a new whole. Her innate preference to continually search and attempt to integrate new services into her realm is a distinct advantage to you, the salesperson. And she may tell you new ways, even some you have not even thought of, in which your service will benefit her. And when she does, stop pushing your traditional benefits and help her develop her own. She may also tell you ways to tweak your service to meet her needs that increase your profitability. Instead of trying to get her "back on track" with your presentation, let her brainstorm—remember, she thinks out loud—and come up with a customized solution.

In many sales presentations, there will be decision makers or influencers meeting you for the first time. In a B2B sale, members of her team will most likely be present, and in my financial-planner example, here's when you will meet her husband or partner. Most likely it will be a mixed-gender group. So now what do you do? It's your job to convince everyone in the room. You need to use the skills you have learned in *The X and Y of Buy* to connect to each person.

During this meeting, ensure that you continue to strengthen your main relationship with your female prospect (remember to continue to use the X of Buy tips from Phase Two throughout the sales cycle, positioning yourself face-to-face with Samantha and focusing on the positive impact your product or service will have on her relationships). Always acknowledge her comments, signaling that you empathize with her situation. If you do not acknowledge a comment, you risk having her interpret your non-acknowledgment as dismissal. Dismissal is the female kiss of death (women abhor being dismissed).

- *Show enthusiasm.* Be excited about your product and the difference it can make for Samantha. Confidence and enthusiasm are contagious.
- *Forget the facts; sell with story.* Open with a story, not facts and figures about your company. Tell a story about a similar client and the impact your product and service had on the people at the client company or on their customers. Or tell Samantha's company or department's story, the accomplishments that they have had to date, where they are, and then paint a vision of where they can be. With D2C, the story should clearly focus on the success another family had through your services and should paint a picture of Samantha's family in the future. Then segue to your role in taking them there.
- *Focus on them.* I hate to tell you, but even in the presentation phase, Samantha doesn't really care about you or your company. She doesn't care that your company was founded in 1972 or about the product being first manufactured in the founder's garage. She cares about *herself, the people in her department, her company, her clients, her family,* and *her influence.* And Samantha's associates, the others who weigh in

on the final decision to buy or not buy, also care first about their own needs and performances. So stop focusing on you and your company. The presentation is not about you—it is about the people in that room. Your job is to convince them that you care about each of them. And the only way to be convincing is to actually care.

- *Confirm the current situation.* After opening with a story, say to everyone in the group, "When I met with Samantha last week, she outlined your goals of 1. ____, 2. ____, and 3. ____. She also said these are the obstacles that you are facing: 1. ____, 2. ____, and 3. ____ . Just to make sure that I address everything today . . . Samantha, have I missed anything? Does anyone else see something that needs to be addressed or a key factor that I have missed?" By including this second step in your presentation, you confirm that you listened to Samantha, that you want others' input, and that you will continue to be flexible to changing needs and to others' perceptions.

- *Focus on benefits, not features.* During your presentation, focus on the benefits of your product or service. Benefits are different from features, which are characteristics such as size, color, and functionality. "This computer program will double your A/P department's efficiency and take a lot of stress out of the payment process." Benefits answer the customer's question: "What's in it for me?" Benefits are what *cause people to buy*. Women value relationships above all. Stress the positive effects that your product or service will have on her relationships, as well as the relationship that you and your team will form with her team or nest.

- *Use vivid relationship words.* To resonate with Samantha and the other women in the presentation, use relationship words. (To learn to connect well with the men in the group, read the next chapter.) *Collaborate, harmony, efficiency, improved service, employee focused, customer focused, cooperation,* and *dependable* are words that portray building better relationships.

- *Spotlight your expert team.* Have you ever been the prospect in a presentation where the salesperson brings in a team of experts from his company and then never lets them talk? I don't care how charming you are or how exciting your product is; it is boring to hear one person speak for more than ten minutes, much less an hour. When you bring others from your team to participate in the presentation, by all means engage them with a question that shows off their expertise. It's your opportunity to show the depth of your company and of your collective strength. Many times salespeople don't realize that not everyone is going to relate to them. The prospect's VP of technology might not be impressed with you, but when your company IT geek speaks up, it could clinch the sale.

- *Engage every member of the customer's team.* Ask questions and engage all of the customer participants in the meeting. Don't make the mistake of concentrating on just the decision maker, or the person you think is the decision maker. Any influencer can kill the deal. Make sure that each person feels that he or she is involved in the solution. You will actually win points from your female decision maker by getting her entire team to participate in the decision. Your job is to have the customer own the solution. It's *their* solution, not your solution.

- *Close by summarizing and suggesting a call to action.* This is your time to articulate a clear and concise solution. The only thing you need to move forward is her yes. Remember, Samantha prefers to synthesize and empathize. She wants to understand how her decision will impact everyone it touches. If you have been diligently paying attention, you can summarize this for her. Stress that your solution will positively impact her coworkers and her customers. If any stakeholder will be negatively impacted, state that clearly and articulate an action plan to minimize the negative impact. She wants to know you empathize with her situation as well as anyone who is hindered by the change your service or product will lead to. Ignoring or minimizing a negative consequence will jeopardize her trust in you. Better to address it honestly with a clear statement:

"While we have outlined the many positive ways that ABC's services will impact your department, we have also discovered that during the three months of implementation, your department will be running two systems simultaneously. Our ABC team will allocate two full-time customer service representatives specifically to your department during this period of time so that you have extra hands and feet to accomplish the additional work necessary during the transition and do not become bogged down."

Her next step may be to make a final decision, or it may be to gain clarification or more information. State clearly when you can respond with any additional information while acknowledging when you need a decision to execute her timeline.

"As we have agreed in the implementation plan, in order to meet your go-live goal in July, we would need a decision by May 1. You have asked us for a list of the implementation team and the equipment installation requirements. We can get those to you on Monday. Does that give you enough time to decide by May 1?"

PHASE FOUR: YOU'RE OVERCOMING OBJECTIONS;
SHE IS SEEKING ASSURANCE

During any phase of GenderCycle Selling™, you may encounter an obstacle: *the objection*. Objections are a prospect's statements that disclose why she *might not* buy your product or service. It may be a statement such as, "I don't need that service right now," or, "I already buy those products from . . ."

Remember that a woman will work through her decision by talking. So as long as Samantha is talking to you, you're still in the hunt. Consider that she is talking through the situation in order to seek assurance that you and your product are a perfect fit. Here are some tips for giving her that confidence.

- *Welcome an objection as a way to bond.* Don't fear an objection; it's a natural part of Samantha's buying process. She needs to assess her risks, then mitigate them. When she objects, ask yourself, "What is her risk? What damage could our services bring to her relationships? How can I mitigate or eliminate that damage?"
- *Anticipate objections.* Rehearse answers to standard objections. Learn to ask her questions to fully understand and empathize with her *real* objections or risks. This requires you to know your product or

service and how it stacks up to your competition. If your fee is higher, you must be able to explain what value or return on investment the higher fee brings. Or, for example, if you are competing against a larger or better-known brand, you must differentiate your lesser-known product with more customized service.

- *Treat every objection with respect and diplomacy.* Acknowledge Samantha's objection as legitimate. If it is real to her, it is real to you. You may never come back from dismissing a woman's concerns. Once acknowledged as a legitimate concern, give concrete ways to overcome the objection. Better yet, if you have overcome the same objection in the past with other customers (especially another woman like her), cite the specific example and highlight the harmonious results. For example, if Samantha objects that your price is too high or higher than your competitor's, you have not demonstrated the value of your service. Use her objection to build trust by actually validating her objection—remember never to dismiss a woman— and then clarifying your value: "The fee for our services may seem higher than our competitor's fee. However, we include installation and training as well as continued support by a team that is dedicated to you."

- *Restate the objection so she can hear it.* As demonstrated above, restating the objection may reduce the magnitude of an objection or allows a prospect to modify your statement (really, hers) to get closer to the true objection.

PHASE FIVE: YOU ARE CLOSING; SHE IS SOLIDIFYING THE RELATIONSHIP

One of the most crucial mistakes you can make is failing to recognize signs that your prospect is ready to buy. The following are examples that signal Samantha's objections have been overcome and she is ready to get down to the "how-to's" of implementation:

"How quickly can we be up and running?"

"Give me a total cost and any payment options." (Of course you will give her the total costs of the benefits as well as the values of those benefits to reduce her costs, increase her revenue, or positively impact her team.)

"What maintenance contracts, warranties, or guarantees are included or available?"

"I need a list of references to check." (Remember that she trusts people she knows or are friends of

friends. If you cannot produce one of those alternatives as a reference, then give her a reference who
is a woman like her and shares similar experiences.
These are references she will naturally trust because
she believes they are more likely to understand her
unique needs.)

"My last vendor didn't deliver on time. How
will you make sure that doesn't happen?"

"What other services do you offer? Do you have
the ability to grow with my company needs?"

"When can you give a presentation or demon-
stration to my team?" (This question relates to her
specific department for which she is responsible
and to which she is accountable, or in a D2C, her
spouse or family.)

When you've determined she is ready to decide, use closing questions that imply understanding to move her along:

"Would you prefer the red or blue one?"
"Is it more convenient to schedule delivery in the
    morning or afternoon?"
"To lock in this year's prices, should I date the P.O.
    December 31?"
Then quit talking. Give her the opportunity to say
    yes.

PHASE SIX: YOU BECOME HER TRUSTED ADVISOR; SHE BECOMES THE CHIEF INFLUENCER

Congratulations, you've made the sale. The easy part is over. Now, moving from closing the sale to the ongoing account management is akin to having the wedding and then moving to being a married couple. If brides and grooms reallocated the energy and resources they used planning the wedding to planning the marriage, our divorce rates would plummet. Similarly, if salespeople allocated the same amount of time and energy to account management as they do to closing the deal, sales would go through the roof. Why? Because your three best strategies for growth are:

1. holding on to current business;
2. up-selling current products and selling new products to current customers; and
3. encouraging enthusiastic customers to generate referral business.

Here are some keys for morphing from a mere sales-person to *her* trusted advisor:

- *Schedule face-to-face meetings.* When developing a long-term relationship with a female client, continue to develop the relationship face-to-face—sit across from Samantha at lunch.

- *Actively bond.* Women bond through talking. Your job is to listen and empathize with her and her team. Continue to position your services to maximize harmony with those she influences, emphasizing the positive relationships that are built through your product and the positive impact your product has on the people she cares about—her nest.

- *Make it easy for her to network for you.* If a woman loves your product or service, she will actively promote you. Give her a stack of your business cards and provide her with a prewritten e-mail describing your service, with a link to your homepage and e-mail address. Host a party for her and her friends. Invite her to networking functions or to be a guest speaker on industry panels to discuss your products' applications in her company.

- *When disaster happens, it is your opportunity to shine.* Women know problems do and will happen. So when you have your first major hiccup with your product—and most likely this will happen no matter how much you try to prevent problems—see it as an opportunity to further bond with her. Use these steps, and you and your company will enjoy a *better* relationship with your female client after a problem:

1. *Immediately acknowledge the problem.* Even if she does not know about the problem, and even if you suspect she will never find out, disclose the problem. One of the hardest lessons for children, clergy, politicians, and businesspeople to learn, as evidenced by the nightly news, is that it's not the problem that is unforgivable—it's the cover-up.

2. *Take responsibility for the problem.* The buck stops with you.

3. *State that you will fix it as soon as humanly possible, how you will fix it, and when you expect it to be fixed.* Overestimate the necessary time, as you want to exceed expectations.

4. *Fix it.*

5. *Deliver a full report that includes a process to ensure the problem will not reoccur.*

If you were to face a difficult time in your life, who would you want to be with you for support? Most likely you thought of the few people in your life that have shared other difficult times with you and have honestly empathized and have worked with you through the trials. When a client has a problem or an obstacle, you have an opportunity to bond with her, and she will include you in her innermost circle of trusted friends.

Throughout the ages, women have perplexed men.

Henry Higgins wanted to know why a woman can't be more like a man, and King Arthur asked, "How to handle a woman?" With women now accounting for more than 80 percent of all consumer sales and roughly 50 percent of all business sales, both salesmen and saleswomen naturally want to understand the female decision process.

While women are naturally complex creatures, they place the highest value on harmonious relationships and cultures, collaboration, understanding, and empathy. By attentively listening to her, and acknowledging her beliefs and feelings while emphasizing the benefits of your service to the people for whom she cares and is responsible, you will win a lifelong customer and friend.

THE Y OF BUY

Q: What makes a man a man?

A: The eighty-six genes found on the Y chromosome.

The Y chromosome has only eighty-six genes, compared to close to one thousand working genes on the female X chromosome. Due to this huge discrepancy in actual genetic numbers, many people have wrongly assumed that women are complex, and men are simple.

If men *are* simpler—they are so in a good way. The genetic male makeup is efficient, focused, driven, and fueled to make its mark on the world. And so, therefore, is he.

With this in mind, we'll now explore the male sales cycle, not only from your viewpoint, but, more important, from his. Because if there is only one true tenet of sales to men, it is this: selling is not about you or your product or service—it is about him—your Y customer.

GENDERCYCLE SELLING™: THE Y SALES CYCLE

The traditional Y sales cycle also has six key phases that are focused on what you can do to solidify a male customer's trust and ultimately his business. Virtually every interaction will follow these phases, whether it lasts several minutes or several months. But remember that GenderCycle Selling™ focuses not only on what you do during each phase but also on *what your prospect is thinking* during each of these key phases. By understanding his values, preferences, and thought processes, you can adapt your sales and marketing approach to shorten the sales cycle, close more sales, and build long-term relationships with your male clients. In the GenderCycle Selling™ Y sales cycle:

You're . . .	And he's . . .
1. Prospecting	1. Clueless
2. Questioning and listening	2. Answering and sizing you up
3. Presenting	3. Analyzing and prioritizing

4. Overcoming objections   4. Challenging

5. Closing the sale   5. Conquering a problem

6. Promoted to trusted advisor   6. Becoming the chief

SALES SCENARIOS

For this example, here are your two Y sales scenarios:

The first is a business to business (B2B) and the second a retail or direct-to-consumer scenario. Remember that a B2B sales cycle typically follows all of these steps, and a retail or D2C sale may or may not.

B2B

- You are Lynn, a salesperson for ABC Solutions, a company providing technology networking solutions.

- Your prospect is Ed, the chief technology officer for XYZ Inc., a local provider of personal and corporate insurance services.
- Your goal is to create the shortest path to identifying a qualified prospect and then creating a loyal lifetime client using the Y tools you've learned thus far.

Retail or D2C

- You are Lynn, a financial planner for ABC Solutions.
- Your prospect is Ed, the chief technology officer for XYZ Inc., a local provider of personal and corporate insurance services.
- Your goal is to create the shortest path to identifying a qualified prospect and then creating a loyal lifetime client using the Y tools you've learned thus far.

So let's begin, Lynn. Armed with your knowledge of what makes Ed tick, let's walk through the Y sales cycle.

PHASE ONE: YOU'RE PROSPECTING; HE'S CLUELESS

As was the case as we began the X cycle, here I am assuming that you know your target male market and that finding qualified prospects is the natural first step in the sales process. Step two, then, is to understand his motivating needs and to position your offering as the best strategic solution to meeting those needs.

The following steps will help you connect to your male prospects. But at this point, let's assume that your male prospect, Ed, is clueless. He doesn't know you, your company, or your service and might not even realize that he has a need for your product. To position your product as this man's best friend:

1. Create awareness

Grab Ed's attention with a promotion campaign that

- *moves.* Men see movement.
- *challenges him* to conquer a problem.
- *positions your service* as the only tool he needs.
- *features* him as an independent hero.
- *ranks* him as the winner.

2. Discover his quest:

Once you've identified Ed as a decision maker in his company, you must learn all you can about his unique mission before you approach him. Then at each contact you will uncover more about what makes him tick. When you understand his quest—the mark he wants to leave on the world—you can then plan your sales and marketing approach to position your product or service as a tool for his success.

How do you learn specifics about Ed? As you did for Samantha, search the Internet looking for clubs and organizations to which he belongs and/or plays a pivotal role. Perhaps he belongs to the Chamber of Commerce, sits on the board of a nonprofit organization, or plays in a sports league. You can also tap into your network of friends and business associates. A five-minute conversation with someone who has worked with or for Ed can provide invaluable insight into the institutions that he values most.

3. Make first contact

Once you have identified Ed as your guy, make contact. And again as you did with Samantha, one of your most common initial contacts will be a "cold call" conducted by phone or in person. These tips will help you turn your *cold calls* into *warm male prospects.* Some are more feasible than others, but all have the capacity to remove the awkwardness from a first conversation.

- *Identify his teams.* Determine his alma mater, his clubs, and his past companies or organizations with which he was affiliated.
- *Join up or pay a visit.* If it's feasible, join one of his groups, or

attend it with another member you know. In chapter 8, you learned that men trust people who share an objective group membership. His "in-group" is his team, company, or club. The club may be an industry-specific professional club, alumni group, sports team, Rotary, Chamber of Commerce, or his favorite nonprofit organization. Men trust members of their team and place value on specific roles in an organization. If you can't join and participate for some reason, you can also try to find someone in your company who already belongs. Even if he possesses no sales skill whatsoever, ask your coworker to make the contact with Ed using their shared team as a connection. While this is not as strong as you being a comember, this will at least establish you as an extended member of Ed's team.

- *Know your call objective.* As with Samantha, whether you're aiming to land an appointment or qualify the lead, your goal is to gain permission to move on to the next step.

- *Send a concise letter or e-mail introduction.* Include your Web site link and a compelling reason for speaking with you, the date that you will be calling Ed, and what you'd like from the call. While Samantha needed to feel a relational connection with you through this first e-mail, Ed wants it short and sweet. Here's an example of a concise e-mail to Ed, CTO for XYZ Inc., from you, Lynn, salesperson of ABC Solutions. The "male" language is in italics:

Dear Ed,

I am the program director of *your Rotary Club* and was impressed by *your success* in establishing XYZ as the local insurance leader as reported in today's paper. You obviously have *built* a strong foundation and are positioned to *expand* regionally. My company, ABC Solutions, provides IT solutions to give you the platform to *launch* your services both regionally and nationally. I will call you on Friday, April 23 to discuss scheduling a meeting.

Lynn

- *Make the call.* On Friday, with your notes and your calendar in front of you, make the call.

"Ed, this is Lynn Smith, the *program director* of *your Downtown Rotary Club*. Tuesday I sent information to you about my company, ABC Solutions, in response to the article about your company in Tuesday's paper. ABC provides the best IT *tool* for *launching* your services on a regional and national basis. I'd like to schedule a time when we can talk more about XYZ's growth plans and the *role* ABC can *play* in *achieving your next goal*. Are you available sometime next week?"

The introduction e-mail and opening call concisely state your purpose, establish you as a member of his team, acknowledge his success, use results-oriented words, and thus resonate with this Y prospect.

Notice I still did not open with, "Did you get the e-mail I sent?" Ed and Samantha both will use that mistake as an opportunity to quickly get rid of you.

PHASE TWO: THE FIRST MEETING—YOU'RE QUESTIONING AND LISTENING; HE'S ANSWERING AND SIZING YOU UP

Remember that you are gathering information in this phase. You are merely listening, not yet verbalizing your offer.

By applying the following steps you will discover information you need to accurately position your offering as the perfect solution for Ed, your Y prospect. During this particular phase, Ed is answering your questions and sizing you up. He's deciding if you make the cut for the preseason team. Here's what to do to stay in the game:

- *Assume the position.* During the first meeting you must be friendly and professional. Remember, men like to stand shoulder to shoulder with the game plan in front of them, looking out at the world they will conquer. Picture Ed as the leader or quarterback, and stand as if you are a key player on his team to win the game.

- *Ask questions that resonate with him.* Develop Ed's interest by asking open-ended questions that both encourage him to reveal his current situation and think about possible solutions. Recall that for a woman, you wanted to know her *feelings* about the situations and possible solutions, including how these solutions would affect her team members. Not so with him. Great questions for Ed are:

"The article in the paper about XYZ's growth was fascinating. What key factors contributed to your growth?"

"You are clearly positioned to launch your company to the next level. What steps will have to be accomplished for this to happen?"

"Tell me about the hurdles or obstacles in your way."

"Looking out on the horizon, what would success look like for your company in one year, three years, and five years?"

"What type of legacy would you personally like to leave to your company/department?"

If you are a woman, remember, *do not* interrupt Ed. Interrupting to say, "I know exactly how you feel. That happened to me . . ." may be empathetic to you, but he's not looking for empathy. He wants to finish his point. Be sincere and friendly during the meeting. Humor is a plus for Ed. Just make sure your joke is appropriate and actually funny. (If you don't know, test it out on another guy you trust.)

- **Close with action.** As you successfully did during your first meeting with Samantha, you've avoided talking about your product, solution, or company. Your meeting is drawing to an end, and you've listened to Ed and thoroughly understand his situation. Now is the time to make a final statement that builds rapport and confidence that you can deliver results. Keep it brief, use the same type of Y action words you used in your first e-mail, and keep it focused on him, not necessarily his team.

"Ed, I appreciate your time and enjoyed hearing the XYZ story. ABC is uniquely positioned to work with XYZ to launch your services regionally so that you obtain your goal to become the industry leader in three years. I am going to share the goals and obstacles we discussed today with the experts on my team and develop a plan. Can we schedule a date next week when I can bring my team in and present our plan?"

Once you confirm the time and date, it's time to plan your presentation.

PHASE THREE: YOU'RE PRESENTING; HE'S ANALYZING AND PRIORITIZING

Now is the time Ed will learn that you really listened, have done your homework, and can add value to his efforts and goals. The following are the keys to you making the next cut with Ed and his teammates who may be meeting you for the first time. Remember to continue to use the Y tips from Phase Two throughout the sales cycle, positioning yourself shoulder to shoulder with the men, focusing on the action plan and the legacy it will leave to his department or company. And whatever you do, don't interrupt.

- *Show enthusiasm.* Confidence and excitement are contagious and demonstrate to Ed that you know and believe in what you are talking about.
- *Forget the facts; sell with story.* Begin by either telling a story about a similar client and the results he had, or tell Ed and his team's story, with their current accomplishments and a vision of where they want to be. Then segue to your role in the story. Remember, don't mention "helping" Ed. He doesn't want to be helped. He wants someone who can stand next to him and confidently solve the problem. Be the co–problem solver of the story, not the savior. Your product or service is the tool that he will use to fix the dilemma.

- *Focus on them.* As was the case with your X prospect, even in Phase Three Ed doesn't really care about you or your company. Save the details for later. Ed cares about Ed, *his* department, *his* performance, and *his* company. And Ed's associates—the others that weigh in on the final decision to buy or not buy from you— also care first about their own needs and performance. Don't focus on you and your company. Your job is to convince them you care about each of them.

- *Confirm the current situation.* Assert to everyone in the group, "When I met with Ed last week, he outlined your goals of 1. ____, 2. ____, and 3. ____. He also said these are the obstacles that you are facing: 1. ____, 2. ____, and 3.____. Ed, have I missed anything? Does anyone else have something that needs to be addressed or a key factor that I have missed?" By including this in your presentation, you confirm you listened to Ed, that you value his team-mates' input, and that you will continue to be flexible and creative in meeting their needs.

- *Focus on benefits, not features.* Remember that benefits are what compel people to buy—not features. When selling to a man like Ed, frame the benefits of your service as the supreme tool for accomplishing his goals. "Ed, ABC Solutions can ensure your team/company becomes the leader in your industry in

three years by launching _____, which will drive
_____ outcomes . . ."

- *Use vivid action words.* To resonate with Ed and the other men in the presentation (use the tips in chapter 9 to connect to the women in the group) use vivid action words. *Explore, drive, win, conquer, rapid, bottom-line, outcome, overcome,* and *goal* are words that portray movement and results.

- *Spotlight your expert team.* Because it is boring to listen to one person speak for more than ten minutes, engage your team members with questions that highlight their expertise. This will detail the depth of your firm and give you more opportunity to connect to the diversity of personalities on the prospect's team.

- *Engage every member of the customer's team.* Don't address only Ed. Look at and speak to other members on his team. If one of Ed's key influencers is put off by you ignoring or overlooking him or her, that individual can kill the deal. Make sure that every team member is involved in the solution. You must ensure the customer owns the solution. It's Ed's team's solution that you are merely explaining to them, not your solution to boast about.

- *Close by prioritizing with a call to action.* The only thing you need to move forward is Ed's decision. Remember, he likes to prioritize and act. Do not add any other factors into the decision now. Ask for his business with confidence. Paint a picture of the new future and ask him for a commitment for the next step.

If he needs time or you need to provide him with additional information, make sure you establish the time frame in which you will deliver the information and in which you will need a subsequent decision from him.

"You've asked us for a breakdown of the specific installation costs, and we can get those to you on Monday. For us to meet your launch date of July 1, we'll need your confirmation by May 1."

PHASE FOUR: YOU'RE OVERCOMING OBJECTIONS; HE'S CHALLENGING

Remember that men value self-respect versus self-esteem. While self-esteem is inherent, self-respect has to be earned. And the best way to earn a man's respect is for him to witness you overcoming an obstacle. If you are going to be a key member of Ed's team, and your product an integral tool in his arsenal, he has to trust that you can overcome obstacles. Consider any objection his way of setting the stage for you to prove yourself worthy of being his teammate. Here are the keys to making the most of Ed's objections:

- *Welcome an objection as a challenge to overcome.* Any objection by Ed or his team is a critical testing ground for you. Ed needs to access his risks and then mitigate them. When he objects, ask yourself, "What is his risk and how can I eliminate it as quickly and realistically as possible?"
- *Anticipate objections.* As you did with Samantha, prepare ahead of time for typical objections. When a new one arises, ask Ed and his team questions to drill down to the *real* objections or risks.
- *Treat every objection with respect and diplomacy.* Perception is reality until proven otherwise. Acknowledge Ed's objection and then offer concrete steps to overcome it. As you did with Samantha, offer a past objection that your team turned into a winning outcome.
- *Restate the objection so he can hear it.* Reduce the magnitude of Ed's objection by allowing him to modify the statement and clarify the true objection. This will often make your job of addressing and solving the objection easier.

PHASE FIVE: YOU'RE CLOSING; HE'S CONQUERING HIS PROBLEM

A crucial mistake many make is failing to recognize signs that a prospect is ready to buy. Here are examples that signal Ed is now ready to apply the solution:

"When can we start?"

"What are the payment options?" (Remember that here you will give him the total costs of the benefits and the values of those benefits to reduce his costs or increase his revenue.)

"What maintenance warranties are included or available?"

"I will need a list of references to check." (Remember that he trusts the people in his company, organization, or other alumni of his organizations. Give him people who are references he will naturally trust.)

"What assurances can you give me that you will deliver on time?"

"What other services do you offer?"

When it is clear Ed is ready to move forward, use closing questions that imply affirmative action to move him along:

"Would you prefer the gold or platinum contract?"

"Is it more efficient to schedule installation in the morning or afternoon?"

Once you've posed your active questions, give him the opportunity to say yes.

PHASE SIX: YOU'RE PROMOTED TO HIS TRUSTED ADVISOR; HE BECOMES THE CHIEF

You've closed the deal. Now you must move to the ongoing account management, and the real relationship begins. Don't be shortsighted and undermine the foundation of your business. Remember that regardless of your industry, your three best strategies for growth are:

1. holding on to current business;
2. up-selling current products or new products to current customers; and
3. encouraging current satisfied customers to refer business.

Finally, here are some tips for moving from a mere salesperson to Ed's trusted advisor:

- *Go forth and conquer.* When developing a long-term relationship with a male client, continue to conquer problems shoulder to shoulder—sit next to Ed instead of across from him at lunch. Better yet, eat at the bar area of the restaurant. He'll prefer the position and inherently enjoy the movement behind the bar.
- *Actively bond.* Men bond through shared activities. Golf and sporting events position you next to your client

while sharing an active, emotionally fulfilling experience. Take Ed to a ballgame.

- *When disaster happens, it is your opportunity to shine.* In a man's eyes, you can't earn his full respect until you have stood from a fall, dusted yourself off, and started again. Through the following steps, use your first fall as an opportunity to deepen Ed's respect for you and your company.

1. *Immediately acknowledge the problem.* Even if he doesn't or won't know it.

2. *Take responsibility for the problem.* Don't pass blame for a second. Ed will respect your integrity whether or not he exemplifies it well personally.

3. *State that you will fix it as soon as humanly possible, how you will fix it, and when you expect it to be fixed.* Make sure you don't make a second blunder by overstating how quickly you can fix the problem. If anything, overestimate the time it will take you. Ed will be pleased when it doesn't take as long, and you'll look like a hard-fighting comrade.

4. *Fix it.* If you get to Step 3 and never follow through with this step, Ed's respect for you will drop significantly. He will see it as a sign you cannot overcome a problem. If you can't overcome one, how can he trust you to overcome another? This lack of follow-through will lead to either a lost account or at least a very reluctant renewal.

5. *Deliver a full report that includes a process to ensure the problem will not reoccur.* Make this realistic—no pie-in-the-sky-theories—because your ability to solve ongoing problems is a critical element in the mind of your Y client.

The best people to depend on in tough times are those who have weathered storms of their own. When Ed has a problem or an obstacle, see it as your opportunity to earn a seat at his innermost circle of trusted friends.

While men account for approximately 20 percent of all consumer sales, the percentage rises to roughly 50 percent when considering big-ticket items such as electronics, home improvement, and sporting equipment. Men also control or influence many business-to-business sales. While male salespeople have an innate sense of how to join the ranks of the guys, female salespeople will increase their effectiveness with men by understanding their values and decision-making process.

Remember that men are naturally drawn to action. They place the highest value on independence, results, a determined role, overcoming obstacles, and someone who is affiliated with their institutions and clubs. By actively participating on his team with a defined role that brings results, you will win a lifelong customer and friend.

conclusion

FINAL THOUGHTS
ON THE X & Y OF BUY

In his hit single, *Forever and Ever Amen*, Randy Travis summed up the diverse male and female interests by singing that old men talk about the weather and old women talk about old men.

Since the beginning of time, we can only hypothesize that a man's number one priority has been to concentrate on the external environment—what is going on out there in the world. Notice that the male symbol (♂)actually has an arrow that points out. This outward focus has served the world well, as men have led the way in conquering the seas, new lands, and space.

Instead of focusing the majority of their energy on external factors, such as the weather, women have historically placed the largest value on understanding and influencing human relationships. Women have had the primary duty of raising the next generation safely to adulthood.

Men and women's historic roles and priorities have worked well for our species. We balance and enhance each other well—I hope you have seen this as a primary thread through the book. An equally important thread is that the knowledge and respect of the workings and work of the opposite sex is critical not only to our survival as a species, but also to our economy (and, frankly, our sanity). If those of us who are sales and marketing professionals would become experts at equally understanding our own sex and the opposite sex, there is no ceiling to what we can accomplish. We would have at our disposal the full range of tools and talents for ongoing success and widespread significance. Additionally, politicians, healthcare providers, educators, and clergy of all denominations would do well to recognize the innate and specific strengths of both sexes and begin to empower all individuals to use their unique gifts to better the world.

Q&A WITH THE AUTHOR

I always make time for a question-and-answer session at the end of every speaking opportunity. These prove to be some of the most insightful (and funny) experiences of the events. Since the mind works by association, when I present the X and Y of Buy, audience participants naturally relate the information and stories to their own experiences. Marketers, advertisers, and salespeople are naturally curious people *and* curious about people. I have included the frequently asked questions that follow, as you might be wondering some of the same things.

Q. What sparked your interest in how gender differences affect sales and marketing?

A. In March 2002, while on a layover in the Las Vegas airport with my family, I wandered into the airport bookstore. The newly released hardback *The Wonder of Girls* by Michael Gurian caught my eye. I had been traveling nine hours with my daughters, then ages six and four, and was actually beginning to empathize with species that eat their young. I devoured the book instead of my children. Fascinated by the biological explanations of my daughters' and my own forty-something female behavior, I pored over other books that discussed biological gender differences that affect behavior.

Since I have spent my entire professional life in business development, marketing, and sales, and I have a female-differentiated brain, my brain automatically sifts most information through the "how does this relate to marketing?" file. Hence, the X and Y of Buy idea was born.

Q. How does the brain become either "female differentiated" or "male differentiated"?

A. At conception the human fetus is endowed with one X chromosome from his/her mother and either an X or Y chromosome from his/her father. Between the sixth and eighth weeks of gestation, if the fetus has two X chromosomes, female hormones are released to start forming female organs, including the brain. If the fetus has an X and Y chromosome, a different hormonal cocktail with a double shot of testosterone is released, and the male organs—including a male-differentiated brain—begins developing. During other critical times during gestation, the fetus's brain is "washed" with either male or female hormones. Of course this hormonal "brain and body wash" continues at critical times after birth, most noticeably at puberty.

Q. Why do some men have female-differentiated brains and some women have male-differentiated brains?

A. Biologists have proven a huge spectrum of brain difference among men and among women. So while they study the male and female brains, they also realize that there are certain traits in a female- or male-differentiated brain that an individual woman or man may not have. For example, there are women with female-differentiated brains that may never discuss their feelings, and men with male-differentiated brains that can go on and on discussing their emotions.

Scientists estimate that approximately 10 percent of women have male-differentiated brains, and 15 to 20 percent of men have female-differentiated brains.

Pierce J. Howard, PhD, in his book *The Owners Manual for the Brain*, notes these events during pregnancy that can affect the hormone levels of the unborn child:

- mutations within the chromosomal matter
- major or sustained stress, such as war, rape, or bereavement, which suppresses testosterone
- renal dysfunction, such as congenital adrenal hyperplasia, which produces too much testosterone
- injections, such as when mothers take estrogen for diabetes
- barbiturates (taken by 5 percent of pregnant women from the 1950s through the 1980s)
- an extra chromosome (XXY in a boy yields low testosterone)

Q. Are men with female-differentiated brains gay or women with a male-differentiated brain lesbian? Does this determine sexual preference?
A. Absolutely not. While scientists have determined that homosexuality is genetic, all of the genetic factors have not yet been determined. Furthermore, the vast majority of men with female-differentiated brains and women with male-differentiated brains are heterosexual.

Q: Is there any way to tell if I have high testosterone levels?
A: Amazingly, yes. Just take a quick measurement of your ring finger and compare it to your index finger to get what scientists refer to as your digit ratio. Measure from the bottom crease of each finger to the central tip. While sex hormones in the womb differentiate the male and female

brain, they also affect finger length. The more testosterone that you were exposed to in the womb, the longer your ring finger is compared to index finger. The average digit ratio for women is 1.0, which means that the ring and index finger are the same length. The average digit ratio for men is .98, meaning the ring finger is slightly longer than the index finger.

By using this digit measurement technique, you most likely will be able to confirm what you know about yourself. For example, I have a female-differentiated brain, but my testosterone level in the womb was also high. While I am a natural multitasker, prolific talker, sensitive, and emotional, I am also very assertive. And my ring finger is longer than my index finger.

Q: So why shouldn't men talk about gender differences?

A. Because many women are highly sensitive to someone saying that they can't perform a task or job, or cannot perform it as well as a man. Rightfully so, because many of us have had men and women say or infer this very thing—at my commencement ceremony from graduate school in hospital and health administration, my grandmother turned to my father and said, "She'll make some man a fine secretary."

You are now an enlightened man, but I still do not recommend that you expound on this subject at your next cocktail party or client lunch. It is so easy to be misunderstood.

Q. Are women, "economic buyers," more loyal to their incumbent sales-person or account executive?

A. Women value relationships more than anything. Concentrate on building and maintaining an excellent relationship. Women also like to help others. They will distribute your business cards or forward your Web site to someone who needs the service you provide to help their friend and you.

Q. I am a women who makes 90 percent of my sales presentations to men, who are the final decision makers. What is the best way to approach them and to get them to realize that I am an expert in my field?

A. The best way to win a man's respect is to be the best specialist in a specific role on his team. Think, *What specific expertise can I bring to him and his mission?* Men respect and trust others who are members of their organizations. Belong to the organizations they belong to, and play an active and visible role.

Q. Do your tips work in personal situations too?

A. Yes, almost all of the time.

Q. When coming from a woman, does "maybe" mean "maybe" in dating? :)

A. Sadly, when you ask a woman out, and she says, "Maybe," she most likely is giving you a polite no. Sorry.

NOTES

Chapter 1: Different by Design

1. Marti Barletta, *Marketing to Women: How to Understand, Reach, and Increase Your Market Share of the World's Largest Market Segment* (Chicago: Dearborn Trade Publishing, 2003), 10.
2. Ibid.
3. U.S. Department of Labor, "Quick Stats 2007," November 2007, http://www.dol.gov/wb/stats/main.htm.
4. Linda Tischler, "Where the Bucks Are," Fastcompany.com, Issue 80, March 2004, http://www.fastcompany.com/magazine/80/realitycheck.html (see paragraph 9).
5. Michael Gurian, *What Could He Be Thinking?: How a Man's Mind Really Works* (New York: St. Martin's Press, 2003), 15.
6. Helen Fisher, *The First Sex—The Natural Talents of Women and How They Are Changing the World* (New York: Ballantine Books, 1999), 60.
7. Pierce J. Howard, *The Owner's Manual for the*

Brain—Everyday Applications from Mind-Brain Research (Atlanta: Bard Press, 2000), 219.

8. Rita Carter, *Mapping the Mind* (London: University of California Press, 1998), 71.

9. Howard, *The Owner's Manual for the Brain*, 230.

10. Elizabeth Hill, "The Labor Force Participation of Older Women: Retired? Working, Both?" *Monthly Labor Review*, September 2000: 39–49, http://www.bls.gov/opub/ mlr/2002/09/art4full.pdf.

Chapter 2: Buyoscience

1. Mary Carmichael, "Neuromarketing: Is It Coming to a Lab Near You?" http://www.pbs.org/wgbh/pages/frontline/shows/ persuaders/etc/neuro.html.

2. Fisher, *The First Sex*, 6.

3. Ibid., 7.

Chapter 3: Diverse Drives

1. Thomas Riggs, ed., *Encyclopedia of Major Marketing Campaigns*, vol. 2, (Farmington Place, MI: Gale Cengage, 2006), 1679–83.

2. "'Dove Evolution' Goes Viral, with Triple the Traffic of Super Bowl Spot," *Marketing Vox*, October 31, 2006, http://www. marketingvox.com/dove_evolution_goes_viral_with_triple_ the_traffic_of_super_bowl_spot-022944/.

3. Unilever, "The Dove Report: Challenging Beauty," 2004, www.campaignforrealbeauty.com/uploadedFiles/challenging_ beauty.pdf.

4. Julian Lee, "That Figures: Women Buy When Ads Get Real," *Sydney Morning Herald* (Sydney, Australia), October 3, 2005.

5. "Merrill Lynch Investment Managers (MLIM) Survey Finds: When It Comes to Investing, Gender a Strong Influence on Behavior," April 2005, http://www.ml.com/index.asp?id=7695 _7696_8149_46028_47486_47543.

Chapter 4: What Makes Him Tick, What Makes Her Tock

1. Barletta, *Marketing to Women*, 61.
2. CBRL Group, Inc. (Cracker Barrel), *CBRL Group, Inc., 2007 Annual Report*, http://files.shareholder.com/downloads/CBRL/300622968x0x138082/CFCEF854-DE7F-4422-BB93-D9AE70E4C57D/CBRL-2007 percent 20AR.pdf.
3. See http://www.eq-life.com/story.html.
4. Jena McGregor, "Check Those Impulses," *BusinessWeek*, August 21/28, 2006, 16.
5. Teena Hammond Gomez, "New Office Furniture Caters to Multitasking Women," *The Tennessean* (Nashville, TN), January 6, 2008: H1.
6. Wendy Lee, "Men Put Off Shopping Until the Eleventh Hour," *The Tennessean* (Nashville, TN), December 24, 2007, 1E.
7. "Survey Reveals Many Men Share Secret Valentine's Day Desire," http://www.floramex.com/livalentin.htm.
8. Society of American Florists, "Valentine's Survey Results," http://www.800florals.com/care/survey.asp.
9. "Shopping Trends: Battle of the Sexes," *Time*, Style & Design, Spring 2006, 63.

Chapter 5: Target the Eye of the Beholder

1. Barbara and Allan Pease, *Why Men Don't Listen—and Women Can't Read Maps: How We're Different and What to Do About It* (New York: Welcome Rain Publishers, 2000), 103.
2. Ibid.
3. Leonard Sax, *Why Gender Matters—What Parents and Teachers Need to Know About the Emerging Science of Sex Differences* (New York: Doubleday, 2005), 22.
4. See http://www.dyson.com/about/story/.
5. Barletta, *Marketing to Women*, 32.

Chapter 6: Sense and Sensibility

1. Michael Moe, "Finding the Next Starbucks: How to Identify and Invest in the Hot Stocks of Tomorrow" (Web promo for book of the same title), http://www.findingthenextstarbucks.com/prologue.html.

2. Linda Tischler, "Smells Like Brand Spirit," FastCompany.com, Issue 97, August 2005: 56.

3. Ibid.

4. Ibid. See Martin Lindstrom and Philip Kotler, *Brand Sense: Build Powerful Brands Through Touch, Taste, Smell, Sight, and Sound* (New York: Free Press, 2005).

5. Ibid., 57

6. "Aroma of Chocolate Chip Cookies Prompts Splurging on Expensive Sweaters," *ScienceDaily*, January 12, 2008.

7. Tischler, "Smells Like Brand Spirit," 57.

8. Pease, *Why Men Don't Listen*, 35.

9. Sax, *Why Gender Matters*, 17.

10. Helen Fisher, telephone interview with author, June 15, 2004.

11. Helen Fisher, *The First Sex: The Natural Talents of Women and How They Are Changing the World* (New York: Ballantine Books, 2000), 10.

12. Ibid., 16.

Chapter 8: The Economics of Emotion

1. "Whom Do You Trust?" *Ohio State Alumni Magazine*, November/December 2005, 30.

2. Ibid.

3. Robin Lloyd, "Emotional Wiring Different in Men and Women," LiveScience.com, April 19, 2006, http://www.livescience.com/health/060419_brain_wiring.html.

4. Ibid.

5. Ibid.

6. Nancy K. Dess, "Tend and Befriend: Women Tend to Nurture and Men to Withdraw When Life Gets Hard," *Psychology*

Today, September/October 2000, http://psychologytoday.com/articles/pto-20000901-000021.html.

7. Ibid.

8. Ibid.

9. Ibid.

10. John McManamy, "Depression in Women," McMan's Depression and Bipolar Web, 2002, http://www.mcmanweb.com/article-31.htm.

11. Thomas J. Moyer, "A Way of Life," *Ohio State Alumni Magazine*, March/April 2006, 64.

Chapter 9: The X of Buy

1. Mark Henderson, "X Factor Explains the Difference Between Men and Women: A Double Dose of the X Chromosome Defines Females and Could Help to Treat Diseases," *Times Online*, March 17, 2005, http://www.timesonline.co.uk/tol/news/uk/article429547.ece.

2. Ibid.

3. Ibid.

4. Ibid.

ACKNOWLEDGMENTS . . . AND
CONFESSIONS OF A FIRST-TIME AUTHOR

One gender difference explained in this book surrounds the male and female definitions of success. Women define success as their ability to influence a group of people. Women also credit their personal success to the strength of their networks.

For all of the wonderful roles I have in this life—wife, mother, daughter, friend, executive, community leader, strategist—I am first a woman. And as a woman I will tell you that without my network, the wonderful people who support me, this book would have never happened.

First, I would like to thank my mother, Bay Reid, for

her crucial insights and her critical editing skills. I am blessed to have both her unconditional love and her wisdom to guide me in all of the areas of life.

To my father, Neil Hand, from whom I have learned so much growing up as the daughter of the ultimate guy's guy. It is because of you that I have such enormous respect for men and their innate gifts. And special thanks for your sketches that inspired the Hunter and Gatherer artwork in chapter 2.

For my friends Corbette Doyle and Nancy McNulty, who cheered me on and edited and shared their own stories for this book. Corbette, without you telling me I could do it and making it look so easy—supportive wife, great mom, high-powered executive who awakes every morning at 4:30 a.m. to write—I would never have been crazy enough to try. Nancy, you are the wisest mother I have ever known, and your way with words, both in editing this manuscript and making me laugh at each turn of life, keeps me sane. Thanks for always taking my calls and giving me the best advice for raising my girls.

For believing in me and this book, I thank David Dunham, who brought me to Thomas Nelson.

And finally, I thank my daughters, Ally and Carah, for tiptoeing around the house while I wrote and forgiving me for all the times I asked, "Can this wait? I am writing now." And Phil, my best friend and husband, thanks for picking up the slack, believing in me, and most of all, loving me through this crazy adventure of life. Without you, I would just be a shell.

ABOUT THE AUTHOR

Elizabeth Pace is a business strate-
gist and serial entrepreneur. She has led the growth strategies
of three successful venture capital startups, a publicly traded
biotech company, and a five-hospital nonprofit healthcare
system. She is a frequent keynote speaker for corporations
and associations and a lecturer at universities.

Elizabeth lives in Brentwood, Tennessee with her husband and their two children. She invites you to e-mail her
and visit her Web site www.elizabethpace.com.

INDEX